MANNA
FOODS OF
THE FRONTIER

BY
GERTRUDE HARRIS

DRAWINGS BY
HEIDI PALMER

101 PRODUCTIONS
SAN FRANCISCO
1972

Second Printing, October, 1973

Copyright © 1972 Gertrude Harris

Illustrations copyright © 1972 Heidi Palmer

Printed in the United States of America
All Rights Reserved

Distributed to the Book Trade in the United States
by Charles Scribner's Sons, New York

Distributed in Canada
by Van Nostrand Reinhold Ltd., Scarborough, Ontario

Library of Congress Catalog Card Number 72-77565

PUBLISHED BY 101 PRODUCTIONS
834 Mission Street
San Francisco, California 94103

CONTENTS

PREFACE

The frontier exists for anyone with an inquiring mind, a healthy curiosity and the will to experiment. Its basic ingredient is a pristine ecological order; disrupt that order and the frontier moves on. A frontier may exist even within one. It may be here or on Alpha Centauri, but that order is still the prime factor.

When housekeeping methods were primitive and incredibly arduous, women fought for any means to save health, energy and time, at any price. Our mechanized society is the result of that sometimes indiscriminate battle, but we have indeed cut labor waste to an infinitesimal fraction of what it once was. With our army of mechanical servants, living in wilderness is now possible and, even by our standards, very worthwhile.

The current passion to reverse the ecological confusion of our world and return it to its original purity is creditable, but how to realistically attain that goal? Have we gone too far? Not if we remember that kindness is the ability to be involved.

Our old cookbooks advise us that game be bought with "fur and feathers visible." As far as possible this precept should apply to every facet of living; all mysterious and masked components should be shunned. A pint of the finest mayonnaise made with the purest ingredients available can be fixed in fifteen minutes with a bowl and table fork; it takes that long to get to the market and buy a mixture contaminated with chemical preservatives.

No era in history has been so thoroughly, so intimately documented as the American Frontier period, and as I am not one to hang a plastic-coated copper pan on my kitchen wall, so this is not meant to be a scholarly treatise—quaint as a sampler and useless as a painted stove—on the habits of long dead women. Rather, it is meant as a reasonable workable guide for those who wish to take the first step toward a richer, purer and simpler life.

Gertrude Harris
Richmond, California
August, 1972

INTRODUCTION

Culinary ingenuity has never been more thrillingly demonstrated than during the biblical exodus from Egypt. In the desert wilderness, having eaten all they had brought with them, the ancient Hebrews were "given" a new ingredient—a "fine, scale-like thing, fine as the hoar frost on the ground . . ." It was so unfamiliar they called it *manna*, meaning "what is it?" Moreover, they were told they must use it day after day for 40 years! It tasted, so we're told, of "wafers made with honey" and "coriander seeds," which, it seems, grew wild in Egypt and the Palestinian lands. Scholars were later to write that *manna* "contained the ingredients of every delicious food and suited the taste of all who partook thereof."

Certainly the Bible is the oldest of all cookbooks, for it even describes the way *manna* was prepared and cooked: "And the people went about and gathered it, and ground it in mills and beat it in a mortar, and baked it in pans, and made cakes of it . . ." As they were not to cook on the Sabbath, they were urged to "bake that which ye will bake, and seethe that ye will seethe . . ."

It may be thought impious to compare God's gift of *manna* to the gift of corn, potatoes, tomatoes, and other indigenous plants that the American Indian "gave" to the Europeans so many thousands of years later. Yet all that we now consider food was once wilderness-wild and, like *manna* signified the miraculous to those hungry and almost without hope in a new place.

The first American colonists could well be considered the cultural descendants of those ancient Hebrews, for neither was a nomadic people; each was "going home," as they said. Once settled, they moved with only the greatest reluctance. It was their children, however, bred on the sound and song of their parents' adventures, who were the first to move outward to new land.

For a long time, the colonists huddled along the Atlantic seaboard. In fact, 216 years were to pass between the time of the first landings of European emigrants in 1620, until the first women were to cross the unknown and terrifying regions west of the Allegheny mountains.

In those days of slow and difficult travel, storage space was necessarily restricted to tools for breaking ground and building. Women fought bitterly for a few pieces of cherished furniture and clothing; they secreted in the hem of a skirt or in tiny pockets sewn under a petticoat little packets and bags of seeds, cuttings, herbs and spices. Too often the seeds were no longer viable when planted or did not take to the new soil. That was tragedy indeed, for it was those small, friendly flavors that enabled the pioneer woman to make the unfamiliar flora and fauna palatable.

On a frontier, the primary considerations are food, drink, clothing and shelter. It was fundamentally vital to break ground, cultivate the new land, and "tame" wild plants and animals to discover their potentiality for nourishment and cover. So in the hands of the pioneer the use of indigenous material evolves, expands and takes on the aroma, the savor and the gusto of the culture that bred them. Thus a new cuisine develops, built on the ways of the old and strengthened by the new.

BEVERAGES

All old English cookbooks gave much space to brewing, and on our frontiers, beer, ale and porter, cider and mead were made in every household. Methaglin, Mead, Hydromel and Hippocras are the now-legendary brews most widely made in the early settlements. The first three made use of the abundant wild honey, and the fourth was made in coastal towns where imported wines were available. These delicious brews, however, were abandoned as soon as the ingredients for stronger drinks (grains particularly) and distilling equipment became available.

Note: Remember to lay *all* bottles on their sides and, every few days, give each bottle a quarter turn to keep corks moist.

METHAGLIN

6 quarts soft rainwater
1 quart honey
1/2 tablespoon powdered ginger
1/2 yeast cake
For each bottle:
1 small piece lemon rind
1 small stick cinnamon
4 raisins

In a large kettle mix water and honey until well blended, add the ginger and bring slowly to a boil. Continue boiling until reduced by one-third. Cool and when thoroughly cold, put into a jar and add the yeast. Let stand for 3 days, then siphon off and bottle. To each bottle, add lemon rind (discard the bitter white pith), cinnamon stick and raisins. Cork tightly. Put bottles into a wine cellar or dark, dry, cool place for at least 2 weeks before drinking.

HIPPOCRAS

2 gallons sauterne
  (dry but not sour)
1 gallon chablis
20 cinnamon sticks
4 tablespoons chopped ginger root
5 whole nutmegs, grated
1 tablespoon coriander seed
1/2 tablespoon cloves
4-1/2 pounds sugar
1 quart milk

Spices must be whole, not ground or powdered.
Combine the wines, spices and 1 pound sugar. Set aside for 24 hours, then add the remaining sugar and the milk. Stir well and strain twice through doubled muslin. Bottle and cork tightly.

MEAD

4 pounds raisins
1 teaspoon grated nutmeg
6 cinnamon sticks, broken up
1 clove
1 lemon
1 quart honey
2-1/2 gallons soft rainwater
1/2 cup rose water

Put the raisins through the finest blade of grinder or food chopper. Crush the spices in a mortar and chop the lemon (and peel) fine; do not let juices run off. Combine all these ingredients in a large stoneware crock. Mix the honey and water until amalgamated and add to the spice mixture. Set aside in a warmish place for 5 days, stirring daily. Siphon off the clear liquid (or let drip through a double cloth bag) and add the rose water. Bottle and cork tightly.

Variation: Mead may also be made without raisins or lemon and with only the barest of spices. It is actually an elaboration of the more basic Methaglin.

HYDROMEL
(Fermented Mead)

This was in great demand everywhere for sickness (so they said) or celebration. It is easy to make and uses wild or domestic honey.

12 gallons soft rainwater
30 pounds expressed honey
   (without wax)
2 ounces hops
1 pint wine yeast or
   3 yeast cakes

Mix the water and honey in a great kettle and add the hops. Bring slowly to a boil and continue boiling, skimming steadily, for 1-1/2 hours or until froth no longer appears on the surface. Remove from heat and let cool slowly, then draw off into a clean barrel. Add yeast and set barrel in a fairly warm place to ferment for 8-14 days or until it stops working. (The length of time depends on the weather: the warmer it is, the shorter the fermentation time.) Keep top and bunghole lightly covered to keep out dust and insects. The foam that escapes from the bung should be carefully skimmed off each day and a little more honey and water added every 2-3 days to keep up the level. When fermentation stops, one has a choice of 2 methods to follow:
1) The bung may be driven in and the barrel left to stand for 4 more weeks before using.
2) Strain the liquid through a fine hair sieve into a clean barrel and add 3 more cakes of yeast (or another pint of fresh wine yeast) and let the liquid ferment a second time. After fermentation, drive in the bung and leave the barrel 3-4 days to settle completely. Draw off into bottles, cork tightly and store in a wine cellar or a dark, dry, cool place.
Note: Sometimes nutmeg, cinnamon and ginger or other preferred flavorings were added during the second fermentation.

SWEET AND UNFERMENTED CIDER

"How to Keep Cider Sweet"
"About a 1/2 pint of mustard seed into a barrel of cider will keep it sweet through the entire winter."

Farmer's Almanack 1839

Select only sweet-flavored apples, fully ripe and unblemished, if possible. To prevent fermentation, make cider late in the season. It is best made in a press.

As the juice comes from the press, strain it through wool, or double thickness of cheesecloth, directly into a freshly scalded barrel.

In cool weather, allow the juice to stand for 3 days, but if warm, not more than 1 day. Shake or turn the barrel briskly once a week for 4-5 weeks, then siphon off or draw off carefully (not to disturb sediment) into bottles or gallon jugs and cork tightly. Old farmwives lay the bottles on their sides in sawdust in a cold dark place and turn the bottles often.

HARD CIDER

Eventually, this "sweet cider" may turn to "hard cider," when alcohol forms from the natural sugar. Finally, if left long enough, it will change into cider vinegar when the "mother" forms. To help the process along, leave the cork (or if in a barrel, the bung) slightly ajar to admit air; in a few days it will start to ferment and become "hard" and should be drawn off into bottles.

CIDER VINEGAR

2 quarts hard cider
1 cup dark molasses
1/2 cup yeast

To hasten the process, pour cider in a large jar (about 4-quart capacity), add the dark molasses and yeast and stir vigorously. Set aside in a warm place overnight, when it should start to ferment. Pour off into a stoneware crock and set aside for 7 days, uncovered. Carefully pour off liquid (not to disturb the sediment) into a clean jug or bottle and keep tightly corked and in a cool place.

BEVERAGES

WINEMAKING

The quality of the wine is dependent on the quality of the grape used: fine and very ripe for the first quality, the rest for ordinary use. Usually grapes gathered each day are pressed immediately and juices set aside to ferment. A white sparkling wine is made from black grapes by pressing very lightly in order to avoid absorbing the color of the skins; these are later pressed with greater force for less white wines or added to the red grapes when making red wines. After the juice is poured into a large vat, a surface foam develops which is allowed to thicken before skimming. This is done 3-4 times; but any froth that surfaces later, during fermentation, is promptly and steadily removed. When completely clear, the juice is moved to casks and barrels to finish fermenting and to "ripen," where it usually remains from harvest time until about February, when it is siphoned off from the lees.

When the bubbling of early fermentation has subsided and the liquid is clear and not sweet, it is siphoned off into clean barrels for perfect fermentation.

SIMPLE GRAPE WINE

A good method for making wine at home is to first wash the grapes well and then strain them through a cloth. Squeeze them well, letting the grape juice drip into a crock. Put the skins and seeds into another crock or big enameled kettle, and pour on just enough water to barely cover them. Strain this and add the resulting liquid to the grape juice. Add 3 pounds of sugar to each gallon of liquid and stir to dissolve. Let it stand for 7 days to ferment and skim off the surface froth each morning. On the eighth day, pour into a barrel with bunghole open. Let stand for a full day (24 hours), then cover the bunghole securely, preferably with clay to make it airtight. Let stand for 6 months before siphoning off and bottling. Cork tightly.

There is a more complicated method, but one that is well worth the trouble, for the wine produced will be very fine. Use the best grapes available of any variety desired.

Pick grapes from stems and wash well. Put into a stoneware crock. For each 2 gallons of grapes, cover with 1-1/2 pounds sugar and pour on cold water to not quite cover. Let stand for 7 days, stirring daily. Strain through a cloth bag, into a keg or barrel. For each gallon of juice thus obtained, pour on 3 quarts cold water and 2 pounds sugar. Cover the keg securely to make it as airtight as possible. Fit one end of a hose into the bunghole and the other end in a large jar of water. It must stand this way until the water in the jar bubbles continually (about 12 days) and must not be touched until the bubbling stops (in another 12 days). Do not remove hose but pick up the keg and shake vigorously, then let stand 2 more days. Remove the hose and cork the bunghole well. It must now be left to ripen for 6 months.

After 6 months, siphon off the liquid. Dissolve 5 cups of sugar in a little warm water and add it to the wine. Pour back into the keg, cork the bung and let stand for 8 months more. Siphon off the wine, bottle it and cork tightly. There are actually many other ways to make wine, but for the homemaker these are the easier and will make the best wine for the amount of energy and equipment used.

BLACKBERRY WINE

Since blackberries grow in such profusion in so many places throughout North America, this recipe may prove a welcome change for those having a surplus after making jams and jellies. There are many types both wild and cultivated, known by many names: dewberry, bearberry, blackberry, loganberry and so on; all may be used.

Gather perfect berries when ripe and dry—mid-morning after the dew has dried. Measure them all into a large stone crock and for each gallon gathered, pour on 1 gallon of boiling water. Let cool then mash the berries with the hands or a potato masher. Cover lightly and let stand until the mass has risen and formed a crust (from 3-5 days). Strain through fine muslin or double cheesecloth and measure liquid. For each gallon of liquid, add 4 pounds of sugar. Set aside for 10 days to ripen.

When fermentation has stopped, cover as tightly as possible to make airtight and let stand for 6 months. Then siphon off into bottles, cork tightly and store in a wine cellar, on their sides. Every few days, turn each bottle a 1/4 turn to keep the corks moist. The wine will be ready to drink in 2 months but will keep almost indefinitely.

Note: If you plan to drink all of it within a short time, reduce the sugar to 3 pounds; if meant to be kept for some time, use 4 pounds.

PORT WINE

10 pounds dried black figs
3 pounds seeded raisins
3 yeast cakes
2 quarts lukewarm water
12 pounds granulated sugar

Grind the figs and raisins together and put into a keg or large crock. Put yeast into a cup or two of the water and stir. Add a tablespoon of sugar and stir again. Let stand for 10 minutes and when the mixture bubbles, pour over fruits. Stir well. Pour on remainder of water and sugar and stir again. Set aside in a warm, dark place and stir twice daily for 15 days. On the sixteenth day, filter the liquid and bottle. Seal tightly and keep like other wines. It may be used immediately.

RAISIN WINE

4 pounds seeded raisins, chopped
2-1/2 pounds sugar
juice of one lemon
1 lemon, sliced thin
16 quarts boiling water

Proportions may be halved or doubled, as desired.

Combine the raisins, sugar, lemon juice and slices in a stone crock and pour in the boiling water. Stir vigorously and set in a warm, dry place. Stir twice daily for 7 days. On the eighth day, strain through muslin or double cheesecloth. Bottle, cork and store in a wine cellar or a cool, dark, dry place. It will be ready to drink in about a month and a half.

CURRANT WINE

Where currants grow wild in great profusion, this is a good way to make use of them. It is a delightful drink, much cherished by ladies of another day. This recipe was adapted from *The Virginia Housewife* (1831).

Gather the currants on a bright dry day and pluck them from the stems; weigh them carefully and make a note of the weight. Pour into a large stone crock and, using the hands, crush the fruit thoroughly, leaving not one whole. For every pound of crushed currants, add 1 pint of water. Stir well and set aside for 3-4 hours. Strain out the liquid into a large kettle and for each 3 pounds of currants used, add 1 pound sugar. Stir until sugar is dissolved. Bring slowly to a boil and keep skimming; simmer and skim until no more froth rises to the surface. Remove from heat to a dark, dry, cool place and let stand 16-18 hours to cool before pouring into a cask or barrel. Cover barrel very securely, both top and bunghole, to make it as airtight as possible.
If there are 20 gallons, let stand for 3 weeks before bottling; if 30, it must remain a month, etc. The liquid must be perfectly clear when drawn off to bottle. Put a lump of sugar into each bottle; cork very tightly and keep in a cool place; heat will turn it sour.

PEACH "BRANDY"

Peaches were first introduced by early Spanish colonists in Florida. Very soon after, travelers reported seeing peach trees in many Indian villages clear across the southern part of the country.

The Indians were very fond of them and used them in many recipes.

Use the old-fashioned clingstone peach with white flesh. Choose ripe and perfect fruit.
Peel the fruit by dipping each one briefly into boiling water, then into cold water, to loosen the skins. Peel immediately. Do not pit the fruit.
Put the peeled peaches into a large stone crock or jar in a single layer and cover with a layer of sugar. Follow with another layer of peaches, another of sugar and continue alternating layers until all fruit is used, finishing with a layer of sugar. Add more sugar each day until juices are drawn from the fruit and the sugar is dissolved. Then cover tightly with several layers of muslin; weigh down heavily to be sure the crock is airtight. Set in a cool, dark, dry place for 3 months.
Use a slotted spoon to lift out the peaches carefully. Then strain the liquid through the muslin, twice. Bottle the liquid and let stand for a few weeks. Use the peaches for an exquisite dessert or make into jam.

BEET WINE

A most unusual wine. I've had the recipe so long I cannot remember where it came from, but I have the impression it is Russian in origin.

8 pounds beets, scrubbed
   and chopped
12 quarts water
5 pounds sugar
2 pounds raisins
2 yeast cakes

Boil the beets in 6 quarts of water until very tender. Drain off liquid into a crock. Pour remaining 6 quarts of water over the cooked beets and boil again until the beets turn white. Again drain the liquid into the crock. Now add the sugar, raisins and yeast. Set aside in a warm place for 3 weeks. Strain through double cheesecloth and bottle. Cork tightly and store the bottles on their sides in a cool, dark, dry place. The wine is ready to drink at any time.

RHUBARB WINE

This was extremely popular on all frontiers, for the hardy rhubarb plant, known also as pie-plant and wine-plant, grew almost anywhere. Many women carried the "crown" or off-shoot clump for planting on the new homestead. Families moving into long-abandoned cabins found the familiar pie-plant still growing near the kitchen door. Only the stalk is used; the leaves and root are poisonous.

4 pounds rhubarb
   (about 14 stalks)
1 gallon boiling water
1 teaspoon shredded fresh or
   dried ginger
4 pounds sugar
1/2 yeast cake
3/4 tablespoon unflavored
   gelatin, dissolved in
   1/2 cup water

Wash rhubarb well and cut off leaf end and root flares.
Cut into small dice and put into a large stoneware crock. Add the boiling water and ginger. Set aside for 3 days, then strain through double cheesecloth. Add the sugar and yeast, then the liquid gelatin. Let stand for 2 more days. Then pour into a large jug and cork tightly. Set aside in a cool dark place for at least 3 months, then strain carefully and pour into bottles and cork. Lay on sides as usual with all wine bottles. The wine is now ready to drink.

SACRAMENTO FISH HOUSE PUNCH

Truly a frontier invention, now known throughout the country.

2 quarts water
1/3 cup green tea leaves
2-1/2 cups lemon juice
1 strip thin lemon peel
2-1/2 cups orange juice
1 cup sugar
3 quarts bourbon whiskey
1 quart brandy
1 quart dark rum
1 pint peach brandy

Bring the water to a boil and add the tea, fruit juice, lemon peel and sugar. Steep for 10 minutes, then strain and cool. Add the spirits and let stand for 24 hours. Before serving, drop a large chunk of ice into the bowl and pour on the punch. Makes 25 servings.

BEVERAGES

SACK POSSET

1 cup ale
1 cup sherry
4 cups boiling milk or
  light cream
1 whole nutmeg, grated
1 cup sugar
2 egg yolks, beaten

Heat ale and sherry together and add the hot milk or cream.
Simmer over lowest heat for 1 hour. Just before serving, add nutmeg and sugar and beat in the egg yolks until frothy.

LE BRULO

This Cajun drink was taken after the entire meal was finished and the table was cleared. It was a common practice to extinguish all lamps and set alight Le Brulo! Of course, every Monsieur in Louisiana had a favorite recipe. I have tried a few and this is my favorite:
Cut a large, thick-skinned orange in half crosswise. Remove all the pulp and put 2 lumps of sugar in each orange half. Fill each with brandy and set alight. After a few minutes, pour the brandy into a glass (or drink from the orange half).

BEER

Pioneers experimented with yeasts, using bits of bread to obtain their starters. Hop seed was always the first seed sown in a new homestead: it grew more quickly and covered a fence better, faster and "prettier," so they said, than any other vine. To be at its best, the hops should be picked "with pollen on."
This simple and easily made modern recipe for beer uses the hop-flavored malt that comes in 3-pound cans. A license is required by law to make it at home.

10 pounds sugar
water
2 3-pound cans hop-flavored malt
2 packages dry yeast
2 cups sugar

You will need a 4-gallon kettle and a 15-gallon-capacity crock or vat with 1 gallon markings. It is best to use soft water, distilled water or rainwater, but almost any water will work unless exceptionally hard.
In a large kettle, mix the sugar with 1 gallon water and bring slowly to a boil, stirring to be sure sugar is completely dissolved. Mix the malt with a gallon of water, stir vigorously and mix with the sugar water. Turn off heat and cool to about 80° (add a little cold water, if you wish). Mix the yeast in a cup of cold water to dissolve it and pour into a vat or crock, then pour the sugar-malt mixture over it. Do not add water at this time—not until after fermentation. Set the crock in a warm room with even temperature of about 70° to ferment. When first fermentation is done (about 2-3 days), fill the crock with water to the 13-gallon mark. Set aside for several days. Depending on temperature and other factors, it may take from 4-7 days to "ripen": the color will change as it stops fermenting, from a rather thick tan to a clearer and darker brown, with a little frothing around the edges. A hydrometer will help to ascertain the exact time to bottle the brew. When ready and clear, dissolve 2 cups sugar in a gallon of water and bring to a boil; while still hot, add to the brew and stir to blend. Let stand at room temperature for 2 weeks before drinking.

THE PRAIRIE OYSTER

Obviously, the hangover is not an exclusive monopoly of the space age. This was a favorite morning-after remedy.

4 tablespoons cider vinegar
1 egg
salt and pepper to taste

Break egg into vinegar in a glass. Sprinkle on seasonings. Do not mix or stir. Drink promptly and in one gulp.

TEA AND COFFEE

In isolated areas of the frontier (and few places were not isolated) tea was an extraordinary luxury, not because it was so expensive, but because it was almost unobtainable. However, when it was on hand and not prohibitive in price, it was in constant use by women; men preferred buttermilk, coffee and brews. The women wrote that they longed for a cup of tea and drank it with great relish when fresh water was available.

Actually, it may well be presumed that coffee was the frontier drink—as it was everywhere during and after the Revolution.

Certainly it was the Plains drink for coffee, it seems, covered the flavor of standing water or water heavily impregnated with alkaline deposits so often found on the Plains.

Herbs of all kinds were used as substitutes for teas: balm and all mints and sage particularly. Coffee, on the other hand, had few really good substitutes, though many were tried: "horse beans," yellow beet root, acorns, dandelion roots, for example. They were roasted (like coffee beans) with perhaps a bit of fat (lard, butter, bear fat, etc.) added. Dry brown bread crusts, rye grain soaked in rum, were also roasted and ground, as were peas and barley—the list is long and was limited only by the imagination of the settler. Chicory, of course, was a well-known substitute. The root was cleaned, sliced fine and dried completely; then roasted, adding the bit of fat, and ground as needed. When mixed with coffee, it was in proportion of 1 part chicory to 10 parts coffee. The usual method of making coffee was to use about an ounce of ground coffee (with or without the substitute) to a pint of water. Bring water to a boil and pour over coffee grounds in an ordinary coffee pot; it was then kept at a boiling point until of desired strength.

Clarifying the coffee made in this way was quite a problem and a number of solutions were tried: the white of an egg, egg shells, a rind of salt pork or a tiny piece of dried fish skin. When the coffee pot was taken off the fire, a tablespoon of cold water was floated on the top to settle the grounds.

One wonders what the beverages were like that caused Honest Abe to quip: "If this is coffee, please bring me some tea. But if this is tea, please bring me some coffee."

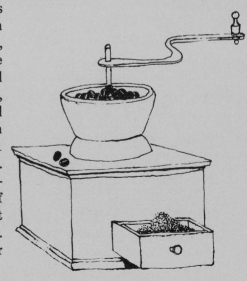

BREAD

BREAD AND HOSPITALITY

On all frontiers, hospitality is not only a gracious gesture but a cardinal rule of life. If there is only bread and water to offer, then it is offered with an open hand and a warm heart.

Hospitality has always been associated with bread. The flat unleavened bread of the desert, the light white bread of the sophisticated city dweller or the coarse whole-grained bread of the peasant and the frontiersman. The bread one knows is the mainstay, the staple of one's diet.

Travelers wrote of the bread-making procedure of the long hunters on the trail: they "opened wide the mouth of the flour bag and a small hollow was made in the flour into which a little water was poured, and the dough was thus mixed in the bag; nothing else was added, except, perhaps, some dirt from the cook's unwashed hands, with which he kneaded the bread into flat cakes, which were baked before the fire or cooked in grease."

Hardtack was carried on the long treks, for it stayed edible for months. It was a dehydrated mixture of flour and water, not very tempting but better than nothing.

Flour, on some frontiers, cost as much as $400 a barrel, notably during the gold rush in both California and Alaska, when the miners made their famous "sourdough." But even at those prices, bread, flapjacks and biscuits were eaten at every meal.

FORMULAS FOR FRONTIER BAKERS

The lessons learned by each generation of frontier people were eagerly sought by successive generations, for in them were the clues to some degree of leisure in a very busy life. Clever homemakers devised and improvised means of reducing the labor; almanacs—the ladies' journals of that day—were read from front to finish for they offered invaluable hints and shortcuts. Rare meetings with other settlers, often of different racial origins, also were helpful, and all these led in time to what is now commonplace in farm and frontier living.

Of course baking was done in a wood oven. Mrs. Lydia Maria Child in *The American Frugal Housewife* (1832) gives the following tip for testing the temperature of an oven:

"Heating ovens must be regulated by experience and observation. There is a difference in wood in giving out heat; there is a great difference in the construction of ovens; and when an oven is extremely cold, either on account of the weather, or want of use, it must be heated more.

Economical people heat ovens with pine wood, faggots, brush and such light stuff. If you have none but hard wood, you must remember that it makes very hot coals and therefore less of it will answer. A smart fire for an hour and a half is a general rule for common sized family ovens, provided brown bread and beans are to be baked. An hour is long enough to heat an oven for flour bread. Pies bear about as much heat as flour bread; pumpkin pie will bear more.

"If you are afraid your oven is too hot, throw in a little flour, and shut it up for a minute. If it scorches black immediately, the heat is too furious; if it merely browns, it is right. Some people wet an old broom two or three times, and turn it around near the top of the oven till it dries; this prevents pies and cakes from scorching on the top. When you get into a new house, heat your oven two or three times, to get it seasoned, before you use it. After the wood is burned, rake the coals over the bottom of the oven, and let them lie a few minutes."

Testing the Unregulated Oven

• Slow oven (250˚-350˚) will turn white flour or unglazed white paper a light straw color in 5 minutes.
• Moderate oven (350˚-375˚), a golden brown in 5 minutes.
• Hot oven (400˚-450˚), a dark brown in 5 minutes.
• Very hot oven (450˚-500˚), a very dark brown in 5 minutes.

Mrs. Child also gives a "receipt" for homemade yeast: "When bread is nearly out, always think whether yeast is in readiness; for it takes a day and night to prepare it. One handful of hops, with two or three handsful of malt and rye bran, should be boiled fifteen or twenty minutes in two quarts of water, then strained, hung on to boil again, and thickened with half a pint of rye and water stirred up quite thick, and a little molasses; boil it a minute or two, and then take it off to cool. When just about lukewarm, put in a cupful of good lively yeast and set in a cool place in summer, and warm place in winter. If it is too warm when you put in the old yeast, all the spirit will be killed."

Obviously, she refers to the keeping of a little yeast from the old batch, to add to the new. A good source of leavening was the lees of wine or, even better, of beer.

MILK YEAST

I find this method very workable.

2 cups sweet whole milk, lukewarm
1 teaspoon salt
1 tablespoon + 1 teaspoon flour

Stir the flour and salt into the milk and set in a very warm place for about an hour, when it is ready for use. This is enough for 1 loaf or a normal batch of biscuits and should be used up completely as it will not keep.

RAILROAD YEAST

From *The American Family Cook Book* (no author, no date). "One tablespoonful of ginger, one teaspoonful of soda, one pint of boiling water; thicken with coarse flour or middlings*; let it rise, and set in a cool place. Use a teaspoonful to a baking of salt-rising bread."

*When flour or corn was ground at home, it was carefully sifted and the various thicknesses were separated from each sifting. This calls for the middle grind, not the coarsest nor the fine.

HOMEMADE
DRY YEAST CAKES

2 medium white potatoes
4 cups water
1/2 cup white flour
1/2 cup cornmeal
1/2 cup sugar
1 cake yeast (compressed)
white flour and cornmeal

Peel the potatoes and cook them in the water until tender. Drain well, reserving water, and mash potatoes fine. Pour the reserved potato water over the flour, cornmeal and sugar and stir well and vigorously; then add the hot mashed potato, blend in thoroughly and set aside to cool to lukewarm. Measure the mixture and add more water if necessary to make 2 quarts. Put aside in a room with normal temperature for 12-14 hours. Stir it down, add enough flour to make a stiff batter, then let rise until very light. Add enough cornmeal to make batter even stiffer, then pat it out to squares about 1/2 inch thick. Cut the squares into 2-inch cakes and spread to dry. Turn them every day until they are hard and thoroughly dry. One cake should make 4 loaves of bread.

SOME LAST WORDS
ON YEAST

• Dried yeast is the most lasting; keep it in a paper bag in a cool dry place. It does not freeze in winter and will not sour in summer; it may lose some of its "spirit" in the heat but may still be used. Keeping it buried in flour is also a good idea.
• *Never*, under any circumstances, *add soda to yeast*. It will never make good, light, sweet bread.
• When using hops to make hop yeast, use the hops that show the pollen dust for that is an ingredient in the rising.
• Yeast will be livelier if a tiny amount—even a ¼ teaspoon— of ginger is added to the dough. More than that may, on the other hand, spoil the yeast.
• Sugar speeds the growth of yeast and salt retards it.
• Cool water also retards the growth, but it does not usually kill it.
• Equivalents:
1 dry yeast cake 2-inch square = 2 teaspoons dry granular yeast = 1/2-ounce cake compressed yeast (standard packaging). Homemade dry yeast cakes are a little slower in action, but the commercial dry granular yeast works as fast as the regular compressed yeast.

BREAD

HINTS FOR BAKING

• Fresh fluid milk and buttermilk must be scalded before using in breads. A factor in the proteins of the whey causes a soft dough and results in poor flavor and texture in the finished product. As evaporated (canned) milk is heat treated during processing, it does not again require scalding.

• The top crust of most "quick breads" and pound cakes should crack so that the loaf may fully rise. This happens because the top crust forms before the center of the loaf reaches a temperature high enough for the action of the leavening agents to be completed.

• To decrease a recipe for four loaves of bread to two loaves, simply divide the ingredients in half. To increase the yield by half, increase all the ingredients proportionately except the yeast. A quantity of yeast sufficient for four loaves will also be enough for six or eight, since yeast action is more rapid in larger quantities of dough.

• Be sure oven is preheated to desired degree before putting in dough to bake.

SUBSTITUTE FOR BAKING POWDER

2 teaspoons cream of tartar
1 teaspoon baking soda
1 teaspoon cornstarch

Sift together seven or eight times and store in an airtight container. The commercial form of baking powder was introduced about 1845 and was immediately accepted as the homemaker's great friend and labor-saver.

BUTTERMILK

Buttermilk has many uses in the frontier kitchen and may be made from a bacillus starter (commercial) or from buttermilk itself. Place a clean glass platter flat on a table and pour a little buttermilk into it. Let dry thoroughly at room temperature and it will form a crust. Scrape this off into an airtight jar and repeat as necessary. To make the buttermilk combine a cup of canned evaporated milk with a cup of lukewarm water (or use 2 cups warm whole milk) and a tablespoon of dry starter. Let stand in a warm place for 2 days, then whip it up light and chill it. Salt may be added, if desired.

MIXED BREAD

"Put a tea-spoonful of salt, and a large one of yeast, into a quart of flour; make it sufficiently soft, with corn meal gruel; when well risen, bake it in a mould. It is an excellent bread for breakfast. Indifferent flour will rise much better, when made with gruel than with fair water."—*The Virginia Housewife (1831)*
I agree entirely; an excellent bread.

BASIC FARMHOUSE BREAD AND CAKE DOUGH
(3 good-sized loaves)

1 large potato
3-1/2 cups water
1 teaspoon salt
2 yeast cakes
1/2 cup lukewarm water
1 teaspoon sugar
1/4 teaspoon powdered ginger
   (optional)
4 cups flour
1-1/2 cups milk, scalded
   (or hot water)
4 tablespoons shortening, melted
2 teaspoons salt
2 tablespoons sugar
   (or molasses, honey, or
   maple syrup)
6 cups flour (approximately)
melted butter

Cook the potato in the water with salt until soft. Cool and peel the potato and return to the water. Mash very well, then strain, saving 3 cups potato water (or add fresh water to make 3 cups).

Dissolve the yeast in 1/2 cup lukewarm water and sprinkle on sugar and ginger. Stir and set aside until foaming and double in bulk, about 10 minutes.

Sift 4 cups flour into a large, deep bowl and make a well in the center. Pour in the yeast mixture and stir well with a wooden spoon. Cover with clean towel and put in a warm, protected place for 1 hour. Then beat in the potato and potato water, milk, shortening, salt and sugar or sugar substitutes; beat in the extra 6 cups flour and continue beating for about 6 to 8 minutes, then move dough to a floured board. Knead until the mass is smooth and satiny and bubbles seem to burst under the surface. Grease a large bowl well and put the dough into it, turning so the entire surface is greased. Cover with a clean towel and set aside in a warm, protected place for 1-1/2 hours. Then punch it down well, re-cover and let rise again until double in bulk. (This latter rising gives the bread a finer texture.) Turn out again on the floured board, knead very well and divide the dough into 3 portions (or 4, if desired). Cover 2 portions while forming the third into a loaf. Put into loaf pans or on baking sheet. Cover the loaves to rise again until double in bulk, about 1 to 1-1/2 hours.

Preheat oven to moderately hot (375°). Brush the surfaces of the loaves with beaten egg yolk and bake for 10 minutes. Reduce heat to 350° and bake for 50-55 minutes more or until done. When tapped with a knuckle, the loaves should sound dull and hollow. Cool on a rack so air reaches all sides of loaves, before cutting. Just before forming dough into loaves is the time to pinch off a cup or so for the next baking; add 1 cup flour and 1 cup water and there you have a simple sourdough starter. Extra yeast will not be needed for next baking.

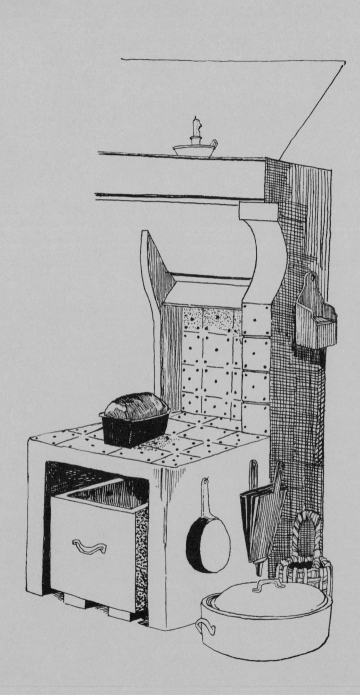

VARIATIONS ON BASIC FARMHOUSE BREAD

This dough can be used as well for white bread, wheat or rye bread, egg bread, as well as a vast variety of coffee cakes and streusels, doughnuts and crusts for deep-dish pies of the old-fashioned kind. The number and variety grows as it is used, experience being the greatest teacher in baking. Following are a few suggestions for further use:

• *Streusel Cake* To make a raised coffee cake, 1 or 2 eggs and sugar to taste may be added to one of the loaves. Raisins, currants, cinnamon all add to the cake flavor. A cupful or a 1/2 cup of melted butter gives richness and delicacy. Rub together 1/3 cup sugar, 1/3 cup flour with 1/3 cup butter until crumbly. Sprinkle over top and press in by hand.

• *Crackling Bread* Blend into the dough: 1 cup pork or chicken cracklings, 1 tablespoon fat from cracklings, 1 teaspoon sugar and 1 tablespoon sour milk. Knead well together, form into a loaf and let rise until double in bulk. Proceed as directed for baking.

• *Rolls* Pinch off handfuls of dough (large or small as desired) and roll into balls. Place side by side in a greased casserole or deep baking dish, or on a baking sheet. Let "rise light" until double in bulk, then bake in a moderately hot oven (375°) until done. Salt may be sprinkled on before baking.

• *Biscuits* Rub a large tablespoon of butter into 4 cups of risen dough. Knead well and form into biscuits and bake quickly.

• *English Crumpets* After the second rising, put 4 cups dough into a deep bowl. Beat 3 egg yolks and blend into the dough thoroughly. Wash the beater very well and beat 3 egg whites until dry and add to the dough. Beat well and add, very gradually, enough lukewarm water to make the batter the thickness of buckwheat cake batter or a heavy cream. Beat for about 10 minutes and set to rise until doubled in bulk.

Have a hot griddle ready and for each 4-inch cake, pour on about 3 tablespoons batter. They do not require turning. There are special crumpet forms to keep them from spreading, but they are not absolutely necessary.

• *Bishop's Bread, Holy Pokes or Huffjuffs* A fine example of the New England penchant for calling things by odd, tongue-twisting names; they were a delight for childrens' Sunday night suppers. When bread dough has risen once, pinch off tiny balls the size of robins' eggs (or large marbles) and let rise again until doubled in bulk. Heat deep fat to about 360° and fry the balls until golden. Pour on plenty of melted butter or serve maple syrup on the side.

• *Crackers* To 1/3 of the prepared dough, beat in 1 cup water until thoroughly blended, then roll out very, very thin. Cut squares or rounds and lay on baking sheet. Prick each in several places with the tines of a fork and let stand for 15 minutes. Bake in a hot oven (400°). Watch carefully that they do not burn; 15-20 minutes should be enough.

• *Braided Party Loaf* Divide each part of the dough into thirds. Roll each third under the palm to make a long rope; pinch 3 ends together and form into a braid, small at the ends and high in the middle. Brush with beaten egg and bake. Braids may also be formed to decorate top of an ordinary loaf.

• *Easy Christmas Coffee Cake or Stollen* Use half of the basic dough for a very generous cake. Form into a large ball, then flatten with the palm of the hand. Mix together 1 cup chopped candied fruit, 1/2 cup raisins and 1/4 cup chopped nutmeats (optional). Put this mixture into the center of the flattened ball of dough, then fold the outer edges inward and over the filling. Knead on a floured board, adding more flour, if necessary. Shape into a long rectangle and fold the dough in half lengthwise. Put on a greased baking sheet, brush with melted butter and sprinkle with cinnamon, nutmeg and powdered cloves.

Let loaf rise in a warm place until doubled in bulk and bake in a moderate oven (350°) for 20-30 minutes. Remove from oven and while still hot, brush with milk or corn syrup and cool on a rack. Sprinkle with confectioners' sugar, for an added touch of delicacy.

IRISH SODA BREAD

1 tablespoon + 1 teaspoon butter
4 cups flour
1-1/2 teaspoons salt
1 teaspoon baking soda
1 cup buttermilk

This bread is easily and quickly made, and delicious plain or as a "tea cake" with some sweetening and currants added. This modern recipe is almost foolproof.

Rub the butter and flour together and add the salt and baking soda. Mix well together with the fingers, until well blended. Stir the buttermilk into the mixture with a wooden spoon and, with floured hands, knead lightly into a ball. Turn out on a lightly floured board and flatten the dough into a circle 1-1/2 inches thick with the palm of the hand. Then, with a sharp and floured knife, cut a cross in the center. Bake in a hot oven (425°) for about 30-35 minutes. Let stand on a rack to cool a little before eating; it is best to break the bread into the four quarters formed by the cross, if it is to be eaten hot. Serve with lots of sweet fresh butter.

IRISH SODA TEA CAKE

1-1/2 tablespoons butter
2 cups flour
3 teaspoons sugar
2 teaspoons soda
2 teaspoons salt
4-1/2 cups white or
   whole wheat flour
2-1/2 cups buttermilk
1 cup currants

Work together the butter and flour and mix in all the remaining ingredients, working as lightly as possible. Roll quickly into a ball and move to the floured board. Proceed as for Irish Soda Bread above.

MIDWESTERN FRONTIER RYE BREAD

2 medium-size potatoes, peeled
3 cups water
1-1/2 yeast cakes
1/4 cup lukewarm water
1 tablespoon sugar
   (or other sweetening)
4 cups rye flour
2 cups whole wheat, white
   or graham flour
1 teaspoon caraway seeds

Boil the potatoes, drain (reserving water in a large bowl) and "rice" or mash potatoes lightly. In another bowl, break the yeast into lukewarm water and sprinkle on the sugar; let stand until bubbly. When potato water has cooled to lukewarm, measure out 2 cups. Add yeast mixture. Measure out 1 cup of the mashed potatoes and gradually beat it into the water with the remaining ingredients. Move dough to a floured board and knead well for about 10 minutes. Let rise in a warm, protected place until double in bulk, then knead again. Now line the large bowl with a well-floured cloth or towel and put the dough into it. Let rise until double in bulk, then invert the bowl over a well-greased baking sheet and let the dough fall gently onto it in a round mass; if cloth sticks, remove carefully. Sprinkle on some caraway seeds and coarse salt, if desired, and bake in a very hot oven (425°) for 10 minutes; reduce heat to 375° and continue baking for 40 minutes more or until done. Makes 1 large or 2 medium loaves.

If real "sourdough rye" is wanted, keep 1/2 or 1/3 of this dough to sour for the next baking.

RICE BREAD

This excellent and unusual bread, adapted from *The Virginia Housewife*, requires no kneading, unless desired.

3/4 cup uncooked rice
4 cups water
2 yeast cakes
1/2 cup water
8 cups flour
2 teaspoons salt
tepid water

Boil the rice in 4 cups water until it is soft and dry; put into a bowl and let cool. Break the yeast into the 1/2 cup water and let stand until bubbly. When rice has cooled to lukewarm, add the yeast and gradually beat in the flour. Beat in the salt and enough tepid water to make the batter workable and the consistency of bread dough. Cover with a cloth and let rise in a warm protected place. When well risen, put the dough into loaf pans and allow to rise once more, then bake in a hot oven (400°) for 10 minutes; reduce heat to 350° and continue baking until done.

MARJORY ANDERSON'S OATMEAL BREAD

2 cups uncooked oatmeal
2 tablespoons shortening
1/2 teaspoon salt
1/2 cup honey
1/4 cup less 1 teaspoon molasses
1 quart boiling water
1 yeast cake
1/4 cup lukewarm water
7 cups flour (approximately)

Put oatmeal, shortening, salt, honey and molasses in a large mixing bowl and pour on the boiling water; set aside to cool to lukewarm. Break up yeast in lukewarm water and let stand until bubbly. When oatmeal mixture is ready, add the yeast and stir in well. Gradually add enough flour, beating in thoroughly, to make a workable dough. Move to a floured board and proceed as for all other bread: knead, let rise, punch down and form into loaves. Put into greased pans, let rise once more and bake in a hot oven (425°) for 10 minutes. Reduce heat to 375° and bake for about 40 minutes more or until done. Cool on racks before cutting.

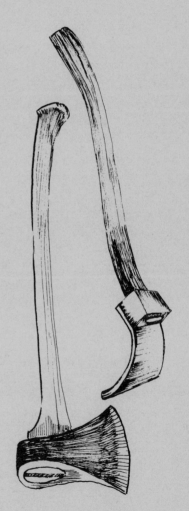

SALLY LUNN

One of the most famous of early colonial breads was the Sally Lunn. It has been said that warm rolls were once hawked through the streets of English cities by girls calling out "Sol et Lune!" (sun and moon) to describe the golden tops and fresh white bottoms of their wares. In America it somehow became Sally Lunn and was baked into a loaf rather than in rolls or buns. One recipe I have for it—and have had long enough not to remember the source, alas—used sourdough bread batter.

"Piece of raised dough size of a quart cup; add 3 eggs, 2 tablespoons sugar, piece of butter size of a small egg. Work it well. Let it rise again and put into large biscuit pan. Let rise very light once more and bake 15 minutes. Cut in squares and serve very hot."

The "raised dough" may be dough from the Basic Farmhouse Bread or Mixed Bread recipes; they will give a richer product.

SOURDOUGH

Both sourdough and the famous salt-rising dough were of great value on the frontier when and where yeast was unreliable. Apparently sourdough was known in biblical times. In the first English translation of the Bible in 1382 by John Wyclif, we read in Matthew 13:33:

"An other parable Jhesus spac to (t)hem, the Kyngdom of hevenes is like to Sourre dow, the whiche taken, a womman hidde in three mesuris of meel, til it were all sourdowid."

The sourdough starter may be made with water or milk, with or without processed dry or compressed yeast.

The earliest form was made of 2 cups flour, 2 cups tepid water and 2 tablespoons sugar, put into a cleaned and scalded stoneware or wooden crock or pail and beaten till frothy. For taking the starter on trips, a wooden pail is preferable, for if it should spill, enough of the yeast spores or germs remain in the wood to activate a new starter. If milk was available, it was used instead of water for it gave a richer product and soured more quickly. Either way, let it get bubbly and sour.

When using the starter, take out what is needed and *always* "pay back" or "freshen" the starter by stirring in until just blended 1 cup water (or milk) and 1 cup flour. *Never* add more than 1 cup of each at one time.

Let it stand at even room temperature for about 3 hours, then set in a cool place. It will keep well for a few days, but it is best to use it at least once or twice a week. Should you wish to increase the starter (or share it with a friend) divide it into 2 equal parts, and to each part add 1 cup lukewarm water and 1 cup flour. Set aside for a day to multiply.

Should the starter change color, examine it carefully: if it is light orange, that's fine, but if it is light green, it has spoiled and must be discarded. Wash the crock well, first in cold water, then in soapy hot water and rinse thoroughly before using it for a new starter.

The starter may even be dried, to carry more easily on journeys. Work into it enough flour to make it solid and dry, then keep it deep in the flour, in a sack or jar.

A TRUE FRONTIER FARMHOUSE SOURDOUGH STARTER

1 cup sugar
1/2 cup mashed potato
4 cups flour
water in which potato
    was cooked

Mix all ingredients together in a wide-necked crock or jar and set aside in a warm place for at least 48 hours. The starter may also be made with other grain flours such as rye, buckwheat, barley, millet, corn, oat, bran or rice. It was often important to conserve as much white wheat flour as possible, for it was the most expensive and difficult to obtain.

A MODERN SOURDOUGH STARTER

2 yeast cakes
    or 2 packages dried yeast
2 teaspoons sugar
2 cups lukewarm water
    or 1/2 cup milk, scalded,
    and 1/2 cup water
4 cups flour

Use a clean and scalded stoneware, pottery or glass container with a wide mouth and a tight cover. Never use a metal container.
Break the yeast up into the crock and add the sugar and water (or milk and water mixed) and stir until smooth. Sift the flour twice, add all at once and beat to a smooth batter. Keep in a warm place for a day and a half, when it should be yeasty and fermented. The first bubbling may have calmed down, but it is still good.

SOURDOUGH BREAD

2 cups sourdough starter
2 tablespoons sugar
1 teaspoon salt
2 tablespoons shortening, melted
8 cups flour (approximately)
1/4 teaspoon soda
1 tablespoon boiling water

Put the starter into a medium-size bowl (warmed previously) and add to it the sugar, salt and shortening; stir just enough to combine. In a large bowl, sift 4 cups of the flour, twice, and make a well in the center. Pour the batter into it and, with the hands, work the batter, drawing in the flour little by little until a workable ball of dough is formed. Move dough to a floured board and knead in enough flour so it is smooth and elastic, but not stiff. Grease the large bowl well and put the dough in, turning so the entire surface is well greased (to prevent a crust forming). Set aside in a warm place without drafts for about 8 hours or overnight.
Dissolve the soda in boiling water, add to the dough and knead well and thoroughly. Keep folding again and again for about 20 minutes. Again set it aside to rise and when doubled in bulk (about 2 hours), form into 2 or 3 loaves (on baking sheet or in greased loaf pans) and let it rise again for 30 minutes. Bake in a hot oven (400°) for 10 minutes, reduce heat to 375° and continue baking for 40 minutes longer. Remove from oven and cool completely on wire racks before cutting.

SALT-RISING BREAD

2/3 cup milk, scalded
1/2 cup white cornmeal
2 cups lukewarm water
1/4 teaspoon baking soda
11-12 cups sifted flour
2 cups boiling water
4 tablespoons shortening
1 tablespoon salt
2 tablespoons sugar

Add cornmeal to the scalded milk and beat thoroughly. Cover lightly and let stand overnight in a warm place. In the morning it should be light, spongy and bubbly. If it is not, put container into a pan of hot water (as hot as the hand can bear) and let stand until the sponge is full of bubbles (perhaps an hour).

To the lukewarm water, add the soda and about 3 cups of the flour (or enough to make a thick batter). Add the cornmeal sponge to it and beat well. Place in a pan of warm, almost hot, water and keep in a warm place for about an hour or until very light and full of bubbles. Stir down.

To the boiling water add the shortening, salt and sugar and let stand to cool until lukewarm; add the sponge to it and mix thoroughly. Add enough of remaining flour to make a stiff dough.

Move to a lightly floured board and knead for about 10 minutes, until smooth and satiny. Divide into 3 equal portions, form into balls and cover; let stand for about 10 minutes.

Shape the balls into loaves and put into well-greased loaf pans. Brush lightly with melted shortening and let stand in a warm place for about 1-1/2 to 2 hours or until doubled in bulk. Bake in a preheated hot oven (400°) for about 40-50 minutes. Brush tops of loaves with melted butter just after taking out of oven.

Makes 3 1-1/2-pound loaves.

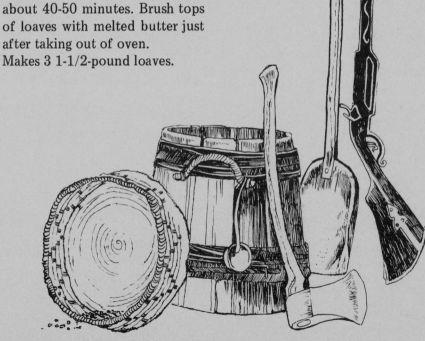

CORNMEAL BREADS

The use of corn on the earliest frontiers supplied the incentive to break with tradition. It is a historic fact that the first planting of wheat for white flour was tragically unsuccessful and the use of corn was necessarily extended for another year; by then it had become a way of life.

Corn proved to be the most vital staple on any frontier. It was the first seed planted on a new homestead and grew anywhere, even on untilled land among the tree stumps. When ripe it could be eaten as a fresh vegetable or dried and used all year. Stored, it did not freeze or spoil and was lighter and easier to pack than potatoes or even rice. For preparing as cornmeal or flour, it could be ground in an ordinary coffee grinder—standard equipment in all frontier homes. The dried corncobs were useful as fuel, and the husks were braided into rugs or tied together with a strip of hide for a broom. The dried leaves were stuffed into bags that served as mattresses.

One of the great pleasures of frontier settlements was the autumn corn-husking parties and most writers of the period left detailed descriptions of them. They were held when the dried leaves of the corn needed to be stripped off. Neighbors for miles around were invited to assemble in a large barn. Each gentleman selected a lady partner, and the husking began: when a lady found an ear of red corn, she was entitled to a kiss from each gentleman present. If a man found one, he was allowed to kiss each lady. When all the corn was husked, the floor was cleared and the fiddle brought out for the dancing which, from all reports, often went on until dawn.

GENERAL RULES FOR BAKING WITH CORNMEAL

• If using sweet milk, add 2 teaspoons baking powder for each 1-1/2 cups of dry ingredients.
• If using buttermilk or sour milk, add 1/2 teaspoon baking soda for each 1-1/2 cups dry ingredients.
• Cornmeal breads are usually beaten much more vigorously than other breads. Baking them in very well-greased iron pans is considered best.

All corn derives from five varieties: dent, flint, soft, sweet and popcorn. Different corns were used for meal in the North and South, which accounts for the different results. The most popular southern type was Boone County White from the dent, while the northern type was flint. Spoon bread is as southern as mint julep and, of course, is made only with Boone County White corn.

For many years, cornmeal or corn flour was simply called "injun" by northern white settlers. "Rye 'n Injun" was the accepted name of a bread using water and a mixture of corn and rye flours or meals. For many it was the staff of life for they never saw wheat bread in any form during most of their lives. Using half corn and half rye flours, or two parts corn to one part rye, it was baked in heavy iron pots buried among the ashes, or on cabbage leaves spread over the floor of the brick oven after the ashes had been removed. The dough could also be patted into a loaf or smeared on a long-handled wooden "peel" (shovel), thrust into the oven then quickly turned and left to bake for an entire day. This produced very heavy crusts, sometimes an inch or two in thickness.

BREAD

SPOON BREAD

5 tablespoons butter
1 cup white cornmeal
1 teaspoon salt
2 cups boiling water
1 cup cold milk
4 eggs

Heat the oven to 425°. Put the butter into an earthenware baking dish or casserole and set it in the oven; the butter must melt completely.

In a large bowl, mix the cornmeal and salt and pour on the boiling water, stirring steadily until smooth. Set aside for 5 minutes, then stir in the milk. Add one egg at a time, beating hard and steadily, and mix in the melted butter. Pour this batter into the hot baking dish and bake for 30 minutes in a moderate oven (350°). This recipe serves only 4 persons but may easily be doubled.

CORN PONES

These were called *apones* by the Indians, who taught the recipe to the white settlers.

When baked in ashes, corn pones were called "ashcakes"; but with buttermilk and soda omitted and baked on a hoe or shovel, they were known as "hoecakes."

3-1/2 cups white cornmeal
1-1/2 teaspoons salt
1/2 teaspoon baking soda
6 tablespoons shortening
   (butter or lard)
1-1/3 cups boiling water
3/4 cup buttermilk (scant)

Sift together the dry ingredients into a bowl and work in shortening with the fingers or a pastry blender, until well amalgamated. Stirring steadily with a wooden spoon, pour on the boiling water. Add enough buttermilk to make a soft dough, just firm enough to handle. Mold into small flat cakes and put them in an iron skillet or on a large griddle and bake in a moderate oven (350°) for about 35 minutes.

SPIDER OR SKILLET BREAD

In the South this was a form of bread, but in New England it had a thin layer of creamy custard through the middle and was served as a cake or dessert.

1 cup cornmeal
2 tablespoons white flour
2 tablespoons sugar
1 teaspoon salt
2 teaspoons baking powder
1 egg
1-3/4 cups milk and water, half
   and half, mixed
1-1/2 tablespoons butter

Sift the dry ingredients. In another bowl, beat the egg and add 1 cup of the milk and water mixed. Stir in the dry ingredients until smooth and pour into an iron "spider" or skillet in which butter has been previously melted. Pour the remaining milk and water over the top *but do not stir in*. Bake in a moderately hot oven (375°) for 25-30 minutes. To serve cut into 8-10 wedges, like a pie.

NEW ENGLAND CORN BREAD

2 cups yellow cornmeal
1/3 cup sugar
1-1/2 teaspoons salt
2 cups sour milk (or buttermilk)
2 tablespoons shortening, melted
1 teaspoon baking soda
1 tablespoon cold water
2 eggs, beaten

In the top of a double boiler (or over very low heat) mix the cornmeal, sugar, salt, milk and shortening and cook for about 10 minutes, then set aside to cool. Dissolve the soda in the water and add it and the eggs to the cornmeal mixture. Pour into a greased baking pan and bake in a hot oven (400°) for about 25 minutes or until done.

Variations: Maple syrup or sugar, molasses or honey may be substituted for the sugar.

A cup of raw chopped apple added to this recipe makes it a fine tea cake.

1 cup crumbled cracklings of pork, ham or chicken skin added makes it a full Sunday dinner. (See cracklings, page 105.)

HOT WATER CORN BREAD

More like a dumpling than a bread this very old recipe from Arkansas was given to me by Mrs. Oralee Knox of Richmond, California. She can remember her grandmother preparing it when she was a child.

1 cup cornmeal
1/2 cup flour
1 teaspoon baking powder
pinch salt
1 egg, beaten
1/2 cup hot water

Sift and blend the dry ingredients into a bowl and stir in the egg. Add the water gradually, beating vigorously. Form into little balls and either steam over cooking vegetables, or bake in a greased skillet.

Variation: Add 1/2 cup of crumbled cracklings for a richer flavor.

HASTY PUDDING OR CORNMEAL MUSH

6 cups boiling water
1 teaspoon salt
1 cup yellow cornmeal

Bring water to a rolling boil, add the salt and slowly pour in the cornmeal, stirring constantly, until the mixture is thick and smooth; bubbles will start to show. If in a double boiler, set over hot water and steam for about 30 minutes; if in a saucepan, turn fire to lowest possible heat and simmer very slowly for same time, stirring frequently. It may be served hot with maple sugar, molasses or honey and hot milk or cream and butter.

Variation: Set aside to cool then cut into slices and fry in hot butter. Or it may be served as a side dish to meat, with gravy poured over. The additions determined whether it would be a breakfast dish, a vegetable, a dessert or a main dish for lunch or supper.

CRACKLIN' BREAD

"She measured the cornmeal from its cloth poke and made 'pones' of dampened meal and cracklings of fried salt pork baking them on hot flat stones."

Anonymous

CORNMEAL SLAPPERS OR FRIED INDIAN CAKES

2 cups cornmeal
1/2 teaspoon soda
1/2 teaspoon salt
2-1/2 cups boiling water
   (approximately)

Mix dry ingredients and gradually stir in the boiling water, adding and stirring until just stiff enough to form into inch-thick cakes with the hands. Fry in hot deep fat—deep enough to come halfway up the sides of the cakes—then turn once and cook until golden brown. Serve with maple syrup and butter.

JOHNNY CAKE

Old-fashioned *johnny cakes* were originally called "journey cakes" though some say they were "jolly cakes." They are as famous in New England as spoon bread is in the South. Some people make them with sugar, some with eggs and even butter; they can be very rich or very plain, but always satisfying.

1 cup white cornmeal
1 teaspoon salt
1-1/2 cups boiling water
   (or half milk, half water)

Mix cornmeal and salt, then pour on the boiling water, stirring constantly until the mixture is smooth. Drop by tablespoonfuls on a slightly greased griddle or skillet. Cook for 6 minutes, turn and cook for 5 minutes longer.

ANADAMA BREAD

This very old recipe from Boston was given to me by Marjory Anderson.

1/2 cup cornmeal
2 cups boiling water
1 yeast cake
1/2 cup warm water
2 tablespoons shortening
1/2 cup molasses
1 teaspoon salt
5 cups flour

Stir the cornmeal very slowly into the boiling water. When thoroughly mixed, add the shortening, molasses and salt. Cool. Break the yeast into warm water and stir to dissolve. When meal is lukewarm, add the dissolved yeast and the flour (enough to make a stiff dough). Knead well and keep in a warm place to rise more than double its bulk. Mold into loaves and let rise until light. Bake at 400° for an hour.

CORN TORTILLAS

Mexican food had a great influence on all southwestern frontier cooking. Tortillas, the mainstay of that diet, were made of flour or *masa harina*, a preparation in which the corn kernels were softened by soaking in limewater to loosen the hulls to facilitate their removal. Then the kernels were ground on *metates*, volcanic stone mortars, with the *mano*, or pestle.

This process was not unlike that of the making of hominy in northern areas. The resulting cornmeal or flour is called masa harina (limed corn, so to speak).

2 cups masa harina
1-1/2 cups warm water
  (approximately)

Mix well masa harina with water and form into small balls about 1-3/4 inches in diameter. The balls may then be put between waxed or oiled papers and rolled very, very thin or they may be—as in Mexican areas—manipulated with the fingers to flatten them, then patted between the palms, pressing constantly, until thin enough. The process is hastened by slapping the flattened round from palm to palm, flattening and turning as it goes. Keep hands moist by dipping into a bowl of water, kept nearby for the purpose. Cook the tortillas on a lightly greased, hot griddle, turning often until quite dry and lightly browned (speckled). Pile them on a napkin, keeping hot, until enough are ready to be served. Butter generously and roll up to eat. Mixtures of meat, vegetables, cheese or other desirable combinations of food may be piled into the tortillas before rolling up. They may also be reheated on the griddle or in an oven, or fried in deep fat for a few minutes, to crisp

ACORN MEAL BREAD

Breads have been made of almost every wild berry and grain found in our wilderness, but the one that seems to awaken the most interest is made of acorns, the seed of the wild oak. American Indians, in all parts of the country, have always made use of acorns. The bread is nutty, rather sweet and very rich.

My own experience with acorn meal being limited, I have asked a young friend, Margaret Lynn Siri, to speak for me here. The acorn bread she describes has been her Christmas gift to friends for some years past, and she made it from the raw acorn right through to the sweet meal.

TO MAKE ACORN MEAL

"To make the acorn flour, the initial task, of course, is to gather and shell the acorns. They are still usable if they have begun to sprout or are slightly moldy. The easiest method I've found to shell them is to literally cut the shell off with a pair of sharp scissors (being very careful to avoid stabbing your fingers). It may be necessary with some hard-shelled species to split the shell by whacking them on the pointed end with a hammer and peeling off the shell. Any way you do it, it's an arduous task. It isn't necessary to remove the inner skins.

"The Indians prepared the acorn meal in numerous ways. 1) The acorns were shelled and buried in marshy ground for several months, then ground and used. 2) They were leached by shelling, grinding and placing meal in a basket left in a streambed where water could run over meal until it was sweet. The reason for leaching is to remove the bitter tannic acid.

"The fastest method is to place the shelled nutmeats in a pan of water and boil them until the water gets dark tea-colored (about 15 minutes), then drain and add more *boiling* water. Keep this up until the acorns are sweet (approximately 2 hours). The length of time depends very much on how many acorns are being done, and the type of oak they come from: some oaks, like the white oak group, have relatively sweet acorns. It is important that a kettle of water is kept boiling so that the change of water is always made with *boiling water*. When done, drain the acorns and spread them in a pan; dry in a warm oven overnight. Finely grind the acorns by running them through a meat grinder, sifting and regrinding the large particles. A better method is to run them through a coffee grinder on a fine setting. The Indians used a mortar and pestle arrangement."

TO MAKE
THE ACORN BREAD

1 cup acorn meal
1 cup white wheat flour
3 teaspoons baking powder
1 teaspoon salt
3 tablespoons sugar
1 egg, beaten
1 cup milk
3 tablespoons oil

Sift together the dry ingredients and add the liquids, stirring just enough to moisten, and pour into a greased pan. Bake at 400° for 30 minutes.

STEAMED BROWN BREAD
FROM ACORN MEAL

This is probably the ancestor of the famed Boston Brown Bread.

1-1/2 cups acorn flour
1/2 cup acorn grits
1 cup white flour
1/2 cup sugar
1 teaspoon salt
1 teaspoon baking soda
1/2 cup raisins (optional, many feel they're better left out)
1/2 cup dark molasses
1-1/2 cups sour milk
2 tablespoons salad oil

Mix all dry ingredients well and add raisins, molasses, sour milk and oil. Dip a pudding cloth in boiling water and wring out. Spread in a round-bottomed bowl and put the batter into it. Tie up the corners and suspend it over boiling water in a closed kettle for 4 hours.

PERSIMMON BREAD

6 persimmons, very ripe
1/4 pound butter
1 cup sugar
2 eggs
1-3/4 cups flour
1 teaspoon baking powder
1 teaspoon baking soda
1/2 teaspoon salt
1/4 cup chopped pecans

In many parts of the South, persimmons grew wild. After much experimentation, the colonists learned to let the fruit ripen until very soft to avoid the mouth-pinching properties of unripe persimmon.

Press the persimmons through a sieve; then add sugar and butter to the pulp. Beat in the egg and continue beating for 4-5 minutes. Sift together flour, baking powder, soda and salt into another bowl, then gradually add it to the persimmon mixture, beating constantly. Stir in the chopped pecans and pour into an 8x11 baking pan. Bake at 325° for 45 minutes.

BOSTON BROWN BREAD
(Without Eggs or Shortening)

1 cup graham flour
1 cup rye flour
1 cup cornmeal
1 teaspoon salt
3/4 tablespoon baking soda
2 cups buttermilk or
    sour milk
3/4 cup molasses
1 cup currants or
    raisins (optional)

Sift the dry ingredients together twice and add the milk and molasses. Stir until well blended then pour into a well-buttered baking mold, cover very securely and steam over hot water for 3-1/2 hours. The cover should also be well buttered and should be securely fastened (or tied down with string) so the rising dough does not force it off. The mold should never be filled more than 2/3 full to allow for rising. It is best to put the mold on a trivet in a large kettle, with boiling water rising to about halfway up the sides of mold.

GINGERBREAD

1/4 pound butter
1/3 cup sugar
1 egg, beaten
2-1/2 cups sifted flour
1-1/2 teaspoons baking soda
1 teaspoon each powdered
    cinnamon and ginger
1/2 teaspoon ground cloves
1/2 teaspoon salt
1 cup dark molasses
1 cup boiling water

Cream the butter and sugar together and beat in the egg. Sift together all dry ingredients. Combine molasses and water. Alternately, combine the dry ingredients and molasses mixture to the creamed sugar. Beat after each addition and beat together until smooth. Line a 9x9 baking pan with oiled or waxed paper and pour in the batter. Bake in a moderate oven (350°) for 45 minutes. Remove from oven and cool for 5 minutes, then invert the pan on a cake plate. Cut into squares and serve with whipped cream, ice cream or a pudding sauce.

APPLESAUCE PUMPKIN BREAD

2/3 cup butter or lard
3-2/3 cups brown sugar
4 eggs
1 cup applesauce
1 cup mashed pumpkin (cooked)
3-1/3 cups flour, sifted
1/2 teaspoon baking powder
2 teaspoons baking soda
1-1/2 teaspoons cinnamon
1/2 teaspoon each mace
    and nutmeg
2/3 cup apple juice
1 cup chopped nuts

Cream together butter and sugar, then add the eggs, one at a time, beating well after each addition. Stir in the applesauce and pumpkin. Sift the dry ingredients together and add alternately with apple juice. Stir in nuts and pour the batter into 2 well-greased loaf pans (9x4x3). Bake in a moderate oven (350°) for 1 hour.

SOURDOUGH PANCAKES

1 cup sourdough starter
   (see page 27)
1/2 tablespoon sugar
2 cups flour
2 tablespoons mashed potatoes

1 cup potato water or milk
   (approximately)
2 eggs, well beaten
1/2 teaspoon baking soda,
   dissolved in 1 tablespoon
   hot water
2 tablespoons butter, melted

It is said if the old "sourdoughs" (the miners) wanted pancakes, they simply opened the flour sack, made a dent in the flour and poured in a cup or so of the starter, some water, salt and a teeny pinch of soda. They stirred up the mess until it "picked up" the required amount of flour, greased a hot griddle, poured on batter and that was all there was to it!

My own method is a bit more complicated, old-fashioned and very rich.

The night before, put the starter into a bowl, large enough for the batter to double in bulk, and add the sugar, flour, potatoes and enough liquid to make it the proper consistency for pancake batter. Let stand overnight in a warmish place.

In the morning add the eggs, soda and butter and beat vigorously until well blended. Heat a griddle, grease with a rind of bacon and drop batter by tablespoonfuls. Brown on one side, then turn and brown the other lightly. Serve hot with syrup or jelly and butter.

SOURDOUGH PANCAKES
(Modern, Quick Method)

2 tablespoons shortening, melted
1 tablespoon sugar
1/4 teaspoon salt
1/2 teaspoon baking soda
1 egg
1-1/2 cups sourdough starter
   (see page 27)

Never use a metal bowl; use glass, pottery or china.

Measure the melted shortening into the bowl and add the remaining ingredients, beating vigorously until well blended, then set aside for about 10 minutes. It should double in bulk; then beat again and drop by spoonfuls onto a hot, greased griddle, turning once to brown both sides. Some like them stacked, 4-5 high; others say they must never be stacked. Serve with melted butter and syrup.

FUNNEL CAKES
(Pennsylvania Dutch)

1 cup + 2 tablespoons flour
3/4 cup milk
1-1/2 teaspoons baking powder
pinch salt
1 egg, beaten
cooking oil
fine sugar

Beat together flour, milk, baking powder, salt and the egg. Beat vigorously with whisk or fork. Heat about 3/4 inch of oil in a skillet.

Holding a funnel (with 1/2-inch spout), put finger over spout opening to close it and pour about a 1/4 cup batter into the funnel. Holding spout over hot oil, carefully remove finger and let batter run out in a stream, making spiral movements as it flows. Fry spirals until golden, turning once with tongs or two forks. Drain on paper and repeat with remaining batter. Stir batter before each addition.

Sprinkle the cakes with fine sugar and serve with maple syrup. These may be stored—without sugar—by cooling completely and putting into an airtight container. Should keep about 2 weeks.

CORN CAKES
(no flour!)

12 ears corn, husks and silks
   removed
3 eggs
1 teaspoon salt
pinch pepper
butter or bacon drippings
   for frying

Grate or scrape corn from ears or, even better, slit corn kernels by drawing a sharp, pointed knife down through the middle of each row. With back of knife, press only the soft pulp and milk out of hulls. Beat the eggs until thick and stir in corn pulp, salt and pepper. Drop batter by tablespoons on buttered medium-hot griddle and cook until tops look dry, then turn and brown lightly. Keep adding butter if needed. Serve on heated plates with warm syrup and melted butter.

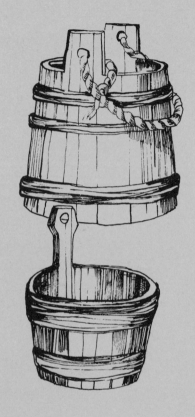

POTATO PANCAKES
(Jewish Latkes)

3 large raw potatoes, peeled
  and grated fine
7 eggs
4 tablespoons minced onion
  (optional)
3 teaspoons salt
1/4 teaspoon pepper
2 tablespoons cracker meal
  (or matzo meal or flour)
fat for frying; about 1/8 inch
  on bottom of pan.

Drain grated potatoes. Beat the eggs and add the potatoes, onion, salt, pepper and cracker meal. Heat some fat in a large skillet or griddle and drop potato mixture by tablespoonfuls. Brown well and turn just once. Add more fat as needed.
These are traditionally served hot with applesauce and sour cream.

IRISH DESSERT PANCAKES

3/4 cup sifted flour
2 tablespoons sugar
1 teaspoon nutmeg
pinch salt
4 eggs, well beaten
1 cup milk
1/2 cup Irish whiskey
1/2 teaspoon baking powder

Combine the flour, sugar, nutmeg and salt. Stir in the beaten eggs, milk and whiskey. Beat very thoroughly.
Let stand 40 minutes in a cool place, then mix in the baking powder. Grease a griddle lightly and fry the cakes, making them very thin.
Serve with lemon and sugar for dessert, rolled up or folded in quarters.

EGGS

Since small domestic animals were brought from Europe with some success, the early colonists soon had an abundance of chickens, ducks and geese. Before that, they depended on the eggs of wild birds and the supply, of course, was seasonal because they could only hunt for them in good weather. Even when there were many chickens, however, the women killed them only with great reluctance, for the eggs were so valued for food —for the sick, to use in cakes and breads, for children, and to put up in a "pickle" for winter use. During the Gold Rush to California, eggs were stored in the flour or meal barrel, to keep them cool and safe.

In San Francisco, the large, speckled eggs of the Murre (or Foolish Guillemot) were found on the Farallon Islands just outside the Golden Gate. The Farallon Egg Company is said to have brought between three and four million of these eggs to San Francisco markets between 1850 and 1856. The eggs were advertised as being "unaccountably large for the size of the bird" and "affording excellent food, being highly nutritive and palatable— whether boiled, roasted, poached or in omelets." An illustration of the egg, in actual size, showed it to be rather narrow on one end and largely rounded on the other and measuring 3½ inches in length and 2 inches at its widest part. The advertisement ran in Hutchings' California Magazine, 1854.

There is little concern in the city with preserving eggs these days, but once it was of overwhelming interest, to judge by the space given it in old books. When living in the country, it is sometimes convenient to buy a large number of very fresh eggs at a pleasant price. Remember that the shells of eggs are porous and absorb light and odors; keep them well covered at all times. They should be refrigerated as soon as possible or somehow preserved for future use. They will not freeze well, but can be kept in "cold storage," i.e., well covered in a dark, cold part of a basement or cellar. An older method was to coat the eggs or immerse them in a solution of "water glass," the popular name for potassium silicate or sodium silicate, which is bought in powder form. To use, mix 1 part sodium silicate with 9 parts water. Pour over the eggs in a large stoneware crock. Eggs must be entirely covered, so put a plate over the top to keep them from floating. In a cool place, they will keep well for 6-12 months, it is said.

It has been found that preserved eggs tend to crack in boiling. To prevent cracking, puncture the blunt end of the egg with a pin before cooking.

TO HARD-COOK EGGS THE MOST FLAVORFUL WAY

Put required number of eggs in a small pan, into which they just fit. Toss on a tablespoon or so of salt and pour on enough tepid water to just cover the eggs well. Bring water slowly to a boil, reduce heat and cook for 11 minutes. Turn off heat and let stand for 15 minutes. Pour off hot water and put under cold water faucet; let water run on them for about 5 minutes (or cover with cold water and add ice cubes). Let stand 10 minutes. Eggs will be perfectly hard-cooked and the shells will come off easily with no evil odor.

PICKLED EGGS

10 hard-cooked eggs
2 cups vinegar
1-1/2 cups water
3 tablespoons sugar
2 teaspoons celery seed
1 small red hot pepper, crushed
1 tablespoon mustard seed
pinch mace
1/2 teaspoon fresh sage, minced
1 teaspoon parsley, minced

Cook eggs and drain; pour on cold water and immediately crack shells and peel. Pack them tightly in a stoneware crock or large jar. Combine remaining ingredients in a saucepan and boil for 5 minutes. Pour while still boiling over the eggs to cover, and seal jar or crock. They will be ready in about 5 days. Once opened, the container should be kept in a very cold place.

WILD ONIONS AND SCRAMBLED EGGS

20 wild onions or green onions
3 slices bacon, diced
6-8 eggs
1 teaspoon salt
pinch pepper

Clean the onions, dry and chop fine (both white and green parts). Fry the bacon dice until almost crisp and remove bacon bits; keep warm. Fry the chopped onions in the bacon fat until soft. Beat the eggs with salt and pepper until beginning to foam and pour over the onions; cook until they set, stirring occasionally. Remove to a warmed dish and sprinkle on the bacon bits.

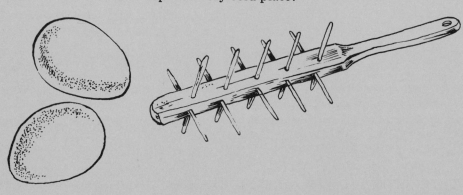

HANGTOWN FRY

One account of its origin is that a miner with a poke full of gold dust entered a restaurant in Placerville, then called Hangtown, and demanded "something different." He was given oysters, bacon, eggs, hot peppers, chili sauce and milk—all dumped into a skillet and fried.

Another account insists the miner asked for the three most expensive articles in the house, to be cooked all together. The result was this recipe:

3 slices bacon
6 oysters
2 or 3 eggs, beaten

Fry the bacon until crisp and remove slices. Fry the oysters until the edges curl, then pour the beaten eggs over them. Cook slowly until eggs are firm. Top with bacon and serve.
Serves 1-2

PIPERADE

The Basques claim this dish as their very own and they might well be proud of it.

3 tablespoons olive oil
1 small onion, chopped
1 tomato, peeled and chopped
1 small green pepper, chopped
1 pimento, chopped
(fresh or canned)
2 tablespoons ham, chopped
4 eggs, slightly beaten
salt and pepper

Heat olive oil and sauté the onion, tomato, and pepper. Add the pimento and ham and cook very slowly for 15 minutes or until all vegetables are soft. Add the eggs and stir in with the vegetables. Cook until eggs have set and turn out onto a hot platter.

EGG PIE

2 cups boiling water
1 teaspoon salt
6 eggs
pepper
1 tablespoon butter
biscuit dough

Pour salted boiling water into a baking dish and break 3 of the eggs into the water. Cover with small balls of biscuit dough and another layer of eggs covered with another layer of biscuit balls. Bake in a moderately hot oven (375°) until golden brown.

OMELET WITH KIDNEY

The following recipe is from *The American Family Cookbook*, unsigned and undated.
"Boil a kidney (beef, lamb or calves') and when cooked, cut it into thin slices. Beat 6 eggs together with 1 tablespoon flour and 1 cup milk, seasoning with a little grated nutmeg and salt. Melt a tablespoon of butter in a frying pan, pour in the omelet mixture and stir it over a low fire until it is firm, then lay the kidney slices on top and fold the omelet over. When cooked, slip the omelet on to a hot dish over which has been spread a folded napkin, and serve at once."

STOCKS AND SOUPS

On most frontiers, soup and meat or fish were simmered all together with whatever vegetables, dried or fresh, wild or domestic, were on hand, and that usually depended on the season. During the long winters great soups were made from old hens, beef, sheep or ox parts, or game such as wild hare, rabbit and venison—even bear's foot, which was, however, much preferred roasted. As to the vegetables, in winter one had only stored or dried vegetables; in spring, one used what was "up." Spices were, naturally, very hard to come by and very expensive when available, but wild and domestic herbs were used with a generous hand.

In old recipes, once the meat was tender and vegetables were added, the procedure was dictated by the form of heat used: "hang the pot high and to the side" meant, of course, a fireplace; "draw the pot to the back" meant a wood stove. Alexandre Dumas, in his cookbook, writes with enthusiasm about what he calls "the eternal pot." I have always called this soup "the everlasting meal," and when I was fortunate enough to have a wood-burning, cast-iron range, such a pot did indeed stand there "at the back" everlastingly.

THE HOT BOX

Most soups and stews are improved when the component flavors are blended in long, slow cooking. To achieve this with a minimum of watching and worrying, the "hot box" came into being. It was a fuel saver (not a small consideration) and, in summer, helped keep the kitchen cool and release the range for more vital chores. After the food has been brought to a boil and cooked for about an hour, it is put—pot and all—into the hot box and left to simmer in its own heat until wanted. If properly made and airtight, the box should hold heat well for at least 12 hours. All country people know its value and it is internationally used.

I first actually saw a hot box on the barge of the Dutch sculptor, Paul Koning. His was made of two wooden packing boxes, one inside the other, the outer being about 4-6 inches larger than the inner one with a layer of cotton batting (unsterile absorbent cotton) carefully stuffed between them; in all, it was about 18-20 inches square. The lid was the fourth side of each box, carefully nailed together with a space between holding more cotton batting and attached by a hinge to the box itself. He used it mainly to cook rice—which he cooked every single day—but also, on occasion, to "finish" his soups and stews.

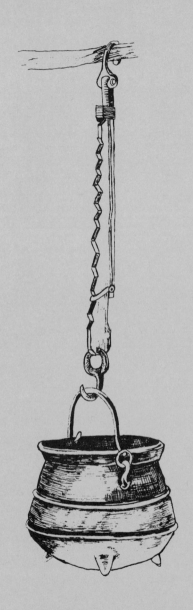

The rice was placed with the proper amount of cold water in a handleless pot. It was boiled vigorously for 5 minutes on the stove, then the pot was put into the hot box and the lid brought firmly down. The rice was ready for use in about 25 minutes, each grain separate, dry and fluffy. Soups and stews were begun on the stove and cooked for about an hour, then put into the hot box and forgotten until wanted. There is, obviously, no chance of overcooking or burning and since no air gets at it, it does not spoil even if left overnight.

A simple wooden box may be used, with hay or hempen rope scraps packed close. A well is formed in the middle of the hay for the pot. Thick newspaper is laid over the pot lid and more hay is wadded over it; finally, a heavy board is laid on top. This is called a hay box.

A more permanent and more elegant version may be made by lining the box with asbestos sheets and painting the outside to match the kitchen decor.

When moving the cooking pot from stove to hot box, do not remove the lid or the heat and steam will escape—and all is then lost. It is that heat and steam that continues the cooking process, for it can get no more in the box.

I have known this pot put to good advantage on a camping trip. In the morning, immediately after breakfast, the soup or stew was prepared and cooked over the campfire. When everyone was ready to take off on the day's explorations, the pot was put into the hot box and never given another thought until we returned, ravenous for dinner, eight or ten hours later. Or, for the first meal away from home, the food can be prepared and partly cooked, put into the hot box to finish cooking during the journey; nothing to do upon arrival but dine in grace.

Any recipe that benefits by long, slow cooking may be done in a hot box. Soups, stews, pot roasts and certain casseroles such as those containing barley, rice, kasha, bulgur and other roasted whole grains.

MEAT AND
VEGETABLE STOCK
"The Everlasting Meal"

3 pounds shank meat and bone
 (shin or other marrow bone)
1 knuckle of veal (optional)
1 old hen (optional)
4 quarts water
2 large onions, 1 stuck with
 4 cloves, the other chopped
3 large carrots, scraped and sliced
2 cloves garlic (optional)
2 small turnips, sliced
3 stalks celery with leaves, sliced
herb bouquet (sprigs of parsley
 and thyme, 1 leek and 1 bay
 leaf, tied together)
1 tablespoon coarse salt

Put the meat (or meats) into a large kettle and pour on the water. Bring to a boil and continue boiling as froth rises to the surface; skim steadily and thoroughly until clear. Reduce heat, cover and simmer for 1 hour. Now, skim off as much fat as possible. A simple way is to sprinkle on a few drops of cold water to bring the fat to the surface. Or, even better, leave overnight in a cool place; in the morning, skim off all fat (it will have solidified on the surface).

Bring to a boil again and skim, if necessary. Add the prepared vegetables and herbs and bring to a boil again. Cook briskly for 5 minutes, then reduce heat and simmer very gently for 2½-3 hours. Or, after 1 hour, place pot into the hot box (see page 45). It will be ready to serve in 2-3 hours.

Other good additions are: parsnips, celery root, leeks and, if eaten promptly, a few potatoes. Be sure to boil and skim after each addition. When adding beans or pastes, like noodles, parboil them separately in boiling salted water. Drain well and then finish the heating in the soup, or put into soup bowl and pour on the soup.

Certain vegetables are absolutely taboo: cabbage, beets, cucumbers, squashes and eggplant among them. If these are required, cook and serve separately.

In many households this stock was preserved all year long and bits of bone and leftover meat, fowl, game and vegetables were constantly thrown into the pot. It meant not only a ready meal but was the basis for many other kinds of dishes: strained and clarified, it could be served clear or creamed, with dumplings, spaetzle, noodles, rice and so on. In any case, the pot was never permitted to be emptied and housewives prided themselves on the age of their stock. If you are not lucky enough to have a stove to keep the stock "in the back of," it should be chilled between uses. Bring to a boil every few days (3-4 at most) to avoid "souring" the soup, and be sure to skim assiduously.

CHICKEN STOCK

Follow directions for Meat and Vegetable Stock and omit beef or veal, though a knuckle of veal and a calf's foot were often added for the extra richness of the gelatin they impart. This makes a clear white or golden stock. Carefully strain through muslin or double cheesecloth, and clarify with the white or shell of an egg. Then add chicken backs, necks, giblets, wing tips and feet, if using the body of the chicken for other purposes. This will make a fine broth.

STOCKS AND SOUPS

FROZEN SOUP

Frozen foods were not as unusual on the frontier as one might think. For soup the method was ingenious indeed. In the great iron kettle a huge amount of soup, thick with meat, fowl and vegetables, was made up and simmered until very concentrated. Then it was carried to an outer area and allowed to get partly frozen. A wooden paddle with a hole in the handle was thrust into the middle of the pot, upright, and the soup was left to freeze solid with the paddle handle sticking straight up out of it. Then it was heated very carefully so that only the soup against the kettle wall would melt and the great mass could be lifted out of the pot. The hole in the paddle was slipped over a sturdy nail in a high beam and there the soup hung until wanted. The desired amount was then hacked off with a hatchet and put into a pot with enough water added to normalize it. It is said the soup improved with time.

GOLDEN CREAM OR PUMPKIN SOUP

1 pumpkin (approximately 2-1/2 pounds)
2 cups water
2 cloves
2 whole allspice
1 coriander seed
1 quart milk
salt and pepper, if desired
2 tablespoons butter
hot croutons

Peel the pumpkin, remove seeds and inner "threads" and cut into large dice. Put into a large heavy saucepan, add the water and spices and cook very gently until pumpkin mashes easily. Press through a strainer and add the milk; simmer for 10 minutes, but do not let it boil. Correct seasoning with salt and pepper. Put the butter in a tureen, pour on the soup and serve toasted croutons on the side.

Variation: A hard-skinned squash will do as well as the pumpkin.

KIDNEY SOUP

Popular particularly in Kentucky, Tennessee and Ohio, the recipe is a very old one, given to me by Miss Mary Greer of San Francisco.

1 beef kidney
2 tablespoons butter
2 medium onions, finely chopped
2 tablespoons flour
1 tablespoon beef extract (optional)
6 cups cold water
parsley, minced

Cut the kidney into 1/2-inch slices. Cut out as much of the fat, pipes and sinews as possible. Melt the butter in a heavy soup kettle and sauté the kidney slices in it; add the onion and simmer until tender. Stir in the flour and beef extract and set aside to cool. Skim off any fat that appears. Blend in the cold water and bring slowly to a boil; cook for 10 minutes. Add the parsley and serve.

With dumplings (see page 58), salad and bread, this makes a full meal.

KENTUCKY PEPPER POT SOUP

Pepper pot soup was a favorite on all frontiers. It varied with the area, of course, but few regions did not have some version. Kentucky Pepper Pot Soup did not become as well known as the Philadelphia variety, nor was it as elaborate. However, it is more typical of most of them.

1 beef shank or shin, cracked
3 quarts cold water
3 onions, chopped
1 cup diced potatoes
1/2 cup chopped celery
2 green peppers, chopped
1 carrot, grated
1 cup corn kernels
2 cups okra, cleaned
2 cups chopped tomatoes
1 tablespoon salt
1 tablespoon chili sauce or tomato or mushroom catsup
1 tablespoon salt
3 tablespoons flour
1 teaspoon butter
water

Put the beef bone and water into a heavy soup kettle; add the onion and cover tightly. Bring to a boil, then simmer for 3 hours. Chill overnight and in the morning, skim well, removing all fat. Prepare the vegetables as directed. Remove soup bone, cut off all meat and dice finely; then return meat to the stock. Add the potatoes, celery, green peppers and simmer until potatoes are soft; then add the carrot, corn, okra and tomatoes and cook gently for another hour, adding the salt about a 1/2 hour before ready. Season with the catsup.

Make a thickening of the flour rubbed with the butter and water. Add carefully to the soup. Boil 5 minutes and serve.

SHAKER HERB SOUP

I begged this recipe at the Pennsylvania Dutch Fair at Lancaster many years ago.

3 tablespoons butter
1 cup minced celery or lovage
4 tablespoons minced chives
4 tablespoons finely chopped
   sorrel
1 tablespoon dried chervil
1 teaspoon dried tarragon
6 cups chicken broth
6 slices toast
grated nutmeg
grated cheddar cheese

In a heavy 3-quart soup kettle, melt the butter and cook the celery until it is transparent (about 3-4 minutes), then stir in the chives, sorrel, and crumbled dried herbs. Cook for 3 minutes longer. Add the chicken broth and bring to a boil. Cover loosely, reduce heat and simmer for about 20 minutes. Taste and correct seasoning, if necessary.

Place the toast in a large tureen and pour soup over it or put a slice in individual bowls and ladle soup on. Sprinkle on nutmeg and a little grated cheese. Serve more grated cheese on the side.

PURÉE OF GREEN PEA SOUP

This was particularly favored in Dutch and German communities, but in one form or another was used everywhere.

1-1/2 cups fresh, shelled
   green peas
3 cups boiling water
1-1/2 teaspoons salt
1/2 teaspoon sugar
2 grinds black pepper
1 tablespoon minced parsley
1 tablespoon corn flour
1 tablespoon butter
2 egg yolks, well beaten
1 sprig thyme
1 teaspoon chervil leaves
   (optional)
mint sprigs (optional)

Cook peas in the boiling water until tender; drain well, reserving liquid. Press peas through a sieve, held over reserved liquid. Stir in salt, sugar, pepper and parsley. Rub together the flour and butter and add to the soup. Bring to a boil, stirring constantly. Blend a tablespoon of the soup with the egg yolks, then pour eggs in a slow stream, into the soup, beating vigorously. Cook for 5 minutes more and serve with herb garnish.

CHESTNUT SOUP

In the crisp autumn when chestnuts hung newly ripe on the great trees, the shovel was kept handy near the fireplace and this recipe was dusted off, to everyone's delight.

2 cups cleaned chestnuts
3 cups cold water
2 cups scalded milk
4 tablespoons butter
1 medium onion, diced
1 stalk celery, diced
2 tablespoons flour
pinch cayenne pepper
nutmeg
salt
1 cup cream

To shell the chestnuts, make a cross with the point of a sharp knife in the flat side of the nut. Put nuts on a shovel and hold at an angle toward the fire. When the edges of the cut curl and the shells come off easily, they are done. Shell them a few at a time, while still as hot as can be handled. Today, a simple way is to melt a teaspoon of butter in a baking pan, add the cut chestnuts and bake in a hot oven until the shells come off easily. Usually takes about 20-30 minutes. After shelling, blanch the chestnuts in boiling salted water and remove the brown inner skin.

Put chestnuts into cold water, bring to a boil and cook until tender. Reserve liquid and press nuts through a sieve; add the scalded milk. In a heavy soup kettle, melt the butter and sauté the onion and celery until soft, add the flour and seasonings and stir well. Add the chestnut mixture and water and cook for 5 minutes. Add the cream, strain and serve.

SORREL SOUP

1 pound sorrel
4 tablespoons flour
1/4 pound butter
2 cups milk, scalded
2 cups cream
4 cups chicken stock
1/2 teaspoon salt
pepper

Wash the sorrel thoroughly, dry and chop very fine.
Blend the flour and butter together and stir into the scalded milk; bring just to boiling point. Gradually pour in the cream, stirring steadily. Add the chicken stock, sorrel, salt and pepper. Cook very gently for 15 minutes, then serve immediately. Stir constantly and do not let it boil.
Variation: Bring 2 quarts of beef stock to a boil and add 1 grated onion and 4 cups chopped sorrel, 1 tablespoon fresh chervil. Bring to a boil, reduce heat and simmer for 15 minutes.

CHOWDERS

A chowder is defined as an American stew or thick soup composed of game, fish or shellfish with salt pork, onions, potatoes, crackers and milk. It is said that the name derives from "La Chaudière," the soup made in France—or by the Basques in Newfoundland. When a fishing fleet came into home port, each boat threw something of its catch into a great copper cauldron and the entire village celebrated their safe return. The two most notable chowders are the New England clam chowder, made with milk or cream, and the Manhattan red, made with tomatoes. So incensed were the New Englanders over this latter version that they once tried to get the Maine legislature to pass a bill outlawing forever the mixture of clams and tomatoes! It did not pass, alas.

NEW ENGLAND CLAM CHOWDER

1 quart clams
6 split crackers
   (pilot biscuits)
1 quart of milk (or 1/2 water)
3 slices salt pork, diced
1 large onion, chopped fine
3 medium potatoes, cut
   in 1/2-inch cubes
1/2 teaspoon salt
dash pepper
2 tablespoons butter

Remove clams from shells and save the liquor. Split the heads of the clams to open them flat; rinse in the clam liquor and remove the black cap. Separate the soft parts from the firm, keeping apart about a cupful of the plumpest clams. Squeeze out the dark part of the bellies. Grind (or chop) the bodies and necks coarsely.

Strain a 1/2 cup of clam liquor. Put the crackers into the milk to soak. Fry the salt pork and remove bits when crisp, then fry the onions. Add potatoes, salt and pepper, and cook very gently, stirring occasionally, for about 10 minutes or until potatoes are tender. Then add the chopped hard clam parts and the liquor, pour on boiling water to just cover and cook for about 20 minutes. Then add the soft clams and cook 5 minutes longer. When the clams are tender, add the milk and cracker mixture, then the butter and simmer for 5 minutes longer. Turn off the heat and let stand on the warm range for about 15 minutes before serving.

CALIFORNIA CIOPPINO

This is the chowder of the Italian fishermen in California. In Italy all such soups are called *Zuppa di Pesce* or "fish soup." Actually, I've heard the same pot of soup called by both names on the same fishing boat. It may be made rather thin and very simple or, as the following, more like a rich fish stew.

3 tablespoons olive oil
1 large onion, chopped
2 cloves garlic, chopped
1 pound tomatoes, chopped
1 teaspoon minced parsley
1 spray wild fennel or anise
salt and pepper to taste
2 cups dry red table wine
2 cups water
2 large or 4 small live crabs
2 pounds firm white fish (striped bass, rock cod, red snapper)
1 pound raw shrimp, with shells
2 teaspoons shredded basil
2 teaspoons minced parsley
slices of bread and grated cheese

In a heavy soup kettle heat oil just until it starts to smoke. Add onion and garlic, reduce heat and simmer until onions are soft. Add tomatoes, parsley, fennel, salt and pepper. Simmer for 10 minutes. Add wine and water; bring to a boil. Drop the crabs into the bubbling soup and cook for 20 minutes. Remove crab; take meat from the shell and crack the claws (for procedure, see page 81), and return meat and claws to the soup. Add sliced fish and cook for 8 minutes. Add the shrimp and cook for 10 minutes. Sprinkle on basil and parsley.
Put a slice of bread into each soup bowl and ladle on soup and some of each kind of seafood.
Serve with grated cheese.
Variation: May be made with only crab or fish or ready-cooked shellfish, removed from shells; 1/2 cup tomato sauce may be added, if desired.

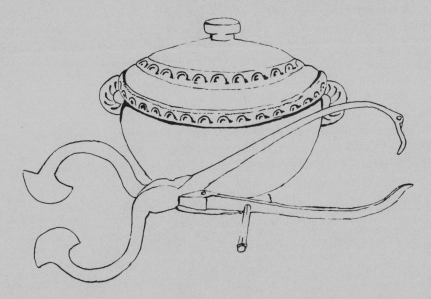

CORN CHOWDER

As familiar as apple pie on the American frontier, this chowder was made of fresh corn, dried corn, hominy or grits.

2 slices salt pork, diced
3 tablespoons butter
6 medium onions, chopped
6 medium potatoes, pared and sliced
2 quarts cold water
6 large soda crackers
1-1/2 cups milk
corn kernels from 6 fresh ears (about 3 cups)
1 teaspoon salt
1/4 teaspoon pepper
1/4 teaspoon dried thyme

Heat a heavy kettle and fry the salt pork until it just starts to turn color. Remove the fried bits and reserve. Add the butter and melt; as it begins to bubble, add the onions and cook until golden. Add the sliced potatoes and water and cook until tender. Break up the crackers in a bowl, pour on the milk and soak for 5 minutes; then pour over potatoes. Return salt pork bits to kettle and add the corn, salt, pepper and thyme. Simmer over low heat for about 10 minutes and serve promptly.

Variation: It was also made very simply by simmering the corn for 15 minutes, pressing it through a sieve and adding 2 cups milk, 1 tablespoon flour, 1 tablespoon butter, then cooking gently for 15 minutes. Salt and pepper were added to taste and it was served immediately.

Pennsylvania Dutch Chicken Corn Chowder was a delicious variation. A chicken was simmered until tender, then boned, the meat diced and returned to the pot. Corn kernels from 8-10 ears were added with a stalk of celery, finely chopped. It was then simmered for about 20 minutes, seasonings added and served with rivels (see page 59), and chopped, hard-cooked eggs sprinkled over.

BORSCHT

The Russians left a powerful heritage in Alaska and Northern California, though their stay was comparatively brief. There is sometimes much confusion about what constitutes a borscht. My Russian-born mother once cleared that up for me: there are many kinds of borscht, most include beets, some have meat, but all are sharply sweet-and-sour in flavor. My own favorite is made with breast of lamb, for it is sweet and tender.

3 pounds breast of lamb (or
   other preferred meat), cut
   in 2-inch cubes
8 cups water
4 cups sauerkraut
2 medium raw beets, scrubbed
1 tablespoon fat
2 large onions, sliced thin
1 bay leaf
1 teaspoon each dill weed
   and parsley
2 carrots, scraped and sliced
2 stalks celery with leaves,
   chopped
1 medium turnip, diced
2 potatoes, diced
salt and pepper
1 teaspoon sugar
2 sausages or frankfurters
1 slice rye bread for each
   serving bowl
Garnishes:
   sour cream
   minced dill
   minced parsley

In a deep soup kettle, brown the meat over low heat (it requires no additional fat if heat is low) then add the water and bring to a boil. Skim if froth rises. Reduce heat and simmer gently.

Rinse the sauerkraut and drain well. Separately, cook the beets in water just to cover until tender, then cool enough to handle; strain liquid into soup and peel and chop the beets. In a large skillet, melt the fat and sauté the onions until soft and golden. Add the sauerkraut, cover and cook for 20 minutes. Add herbs, carrots, celery, turnip, potatoes and chopped beets; stir and cook for 10 minutes, then add to soup. Continue cooking for at least 1 hour more. Stir in salt, pepper and sugar. Taste to correct seasoning if necessary; it may require more sugar or a tablespoon of vinegar or lemon juice. The soup should have a sharp sweet-and-sour flavor.

Skim off all visible fat. If meat is not "falling off the bones," continue cooking. When ready, slice sausages or frankfurters and float on top; heat well. Garnish with sour cream, minced dill weed and parsley. This soup gains in flavor with reheating; be sure it does not burn. This is the typical "back of the stove" or "hot box" preparation and in some Russian homes it is kept going all winter.

Variations: There are more of these than stars in the Russian sky, it is said. Make it with fresh cabbage, with more or less beets, with lemon juice and honey, with a handful of dried mushrooms (after soaking and chopping), with dumplings or a head of fresh lettuce shredded fine and thrown in at the last moment.

CREOLE SOUPS

And finally, there are the gumbos and filés of the Louisiana Creole country that are unique in the story of American cooking: a fascinating blend of the traditional cookery of France and Spain, interpreted by cooks of African origin who used the unusual ingredients indigenous to the area, which they learned from the Choctaw Indians. As early as 1835 they were included in collections of American cookery such as *The Virginia Housewife*, Miss Beecher's *Encyclopedia* and others. There are so many recipes for these, and each a cherished heirloom, that rather than choose one arbitrarily, I have obtained the recipes of New Orleans cooks now in the North. I am very grateful for their cooperation.

TOBEY'S GUMBO FILE

1 old stewing hen
water to cover
4 tablespoons shortening
4 tablespoons flour
8 green onions, chopped
2 cloves garlic, chopped
1 bell pepper, chopped
1 large tomato, chopped fine
2 tablespoons dried shrimp
1 teaspoon salt
1 teaspoon black pepper
1 tablespoon minced parsley
1 bay leaf, crumbled
2 cups sliced okra pods
1 pound smoked link sausages, sliced
1 crab, cracked and cut in serving pieces
1 pound shrimp, shelled and deveined
2 tablespoons butter
12 oysters with liquor
2 tablespoons filé powder
boiled rice

In a 6-quart kettle (or larger), cover chicken with water and bring to a boil. Reduce heat and simmer until chicken is tender. In the meantime, heat shortening in a large heavy skillet and add flour gradually, stirring constantly; cook for 5 minutes or just until flour begins to color. Then add the onions, garlic, bell pepper, tomato, dried shrimp, salt, pepper, parsley and bay leaf; simmer, stirring frequently, for 25-30 minutes. Add the okra pods and cook for 20 minutes longer. Pour this mixture into the large kettle and add *boiling water* to cover. Add the sausages and crab and cook 10 minutes longer. Add the shrimp and continue simmering. Fifteen minutes before serving, heat 2 tablespoons butter in the now empty skillet and add and sauté the oysters with their liquor. Cook until edges of oysters curl. Immediately pour into soup kettle and cook 5 minutes longer. Remove from heat and sprinkle on the filé powder, but do not cook it further, for it makes the soup "stringy." Put boiled rice in individual soup plates and spoon gumbo over it.

ADDIE YOUNG'S
CHICKEN JAMBALAYA

1 3- or 4-pound hen
1/2 cup fat
3 cups chopped onions
1 cup chopped celery
1/2 green pepper, chopped
2 cloves garlic, chopped
6-7 cups water
3 cups raw rice
2 tablespoons chopped
  green onions
2 tablespoons minced parsley
salt and pepper to taste

Clean chicken and cut into small
serving pieces. Heat the fat in a
large heavy Dutch oven and
brown the chicken pieces. Add
the onions, celery, green pepper,
garlic and cook until tender. Add
the water, rice, green onions, seasonings and bring to a boil,
reduce heat, cover pot and simmer very gently until water is
absorbed and rice is dry and
fluffy, about 1 hour.

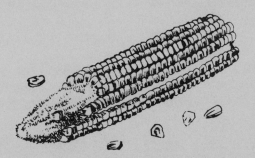

SOUP AND STEW ACCOMPANIMENTS

Dumplings, rivels, spaetzle and other additions were a very important part of frontier cooking. For one thing, they made it possible to stretch food a little further and, for another, they gave the housewife a chance to show off her skill in making them light, fluffy and tasty. They could be made of any kind of flour or meal, with or without eggs, and could be added to soups of every kind. In short, there was no excuse *not* to make them.

SMALL EGG DUMPLINGS

6 hard-cooked egg yolks
pinch each salt, pepper and
     nutmeg
2 tablespoons melted butter
2 teaspoons flour

Mash the yolks until smooth and blend in remaining ingredients to form a stiff mass. Using the hands, roll out tiny balls and drop them into clear, gently bubbling soup, for about 10-15 minutes.

POTATO DUMPLINGS
(Erdapfelknoedel)

3/4 cup bread crumbs
4 tablespoons butter
8 medium potatoes, peeled,
     quartered and boiled
1/4 cup flour
2 tablespoons melted butter
2 eggs, lightly beaten
1 teaspoon salt
pepper to taste
2 quarts salted water, boiling
6 tablespoons butter, melted
2 tablespoons minced parsley

Brown the bread crumbs in the 4 tablespoons of butter, then set aside and keep warm. Put boiled potatoes through a ricer. (It is imperative that potatoes be riced rather than mashed for they must be dry and light.) Mix the potatoes with the flour and 2 tablespoons melted butter, eggs, salt and pepper. Blend thoroughly.
Divide into about 24 little balls and chill for at least 3-4 hours. Then drop them into a large kettle of boiling salted water; bring back to a boil, reduce heat and simmer very gently for 12 minutes. Remove with a slotted spoon or skimmer and drain well. Split each little ball in half and arrange on a hot serving plate. Heat 6 tablespoons butter until it starts to brown, then pour over the dumpling halves. Sprinkle with the browned bread crumbs and serve hot.

EGG FOAM DUMPLINGS

4 eggs, separated
pinch cream of tartar
1/8 teaspoon salt
4 tablespoons flour
chicken broth or stew gravy

Beat egg yolks until light and thick. Whip the whites with cream of tartar until they hold their peaks, then fold into the yolks with salt and flour.
Have broth just under the boiling point in a wide pot; pour in the foamy mixture, cover pot and cook for 3-4 minutes or until the foam is "set" on the top. *(Do not boil.)*
Cut through the foam with a slotted spoon, lifting sections from the liquid, draining as you do. Serve with a chicken dish or with gravy poured over.

SPAETZLE

2-1/2 cups flour or corn flour
1 cup milk
2 eggs
1 teaspoon salt
6 cups boiling water
1 teaspoon salt
4 tablespoons butter
   or bacon drippings
1/2 cup dry bread crumbs

Sift flour into a bowl and make a well in the center. Slowly pour the milk into the well, drawing in the flour gradually to make a smooth creamy batter. Add one egg at a time, beating constantly. Add salt and blend in well.

Pour the batter into a small shallow bowl and tilt it over the hot water. Use a sharp knife; "slice" (or chop) the batter into the simmering water, dipping the knife into the water before each slice, so that the batter does not stick to the knife. Let boil for five minutes, then drain the spaetzle into a colander. Pour into a serving dish and top with bread crumbs that have been browned in butter. Serve hot.

If served as a separate course, applesauce is the traditional side dish.

BREAD CRUMB DUMPLINGS

4 cups beef broth
   (more if required)
4 tablespoons butter
4 eggs, separated
1 teaspoon salt
1 tablespoon chopped parsley
1/4 teaspoon grated nutmeg
2-1/2 cups bread crumbs
minced chives and parsley

Heat broth and keep at a simmer. Cream the butter and add the beaten egg yolks, salt, parsley and nutmeg and blend thoroughly. Add the crumbs and stir well. Beat the egg whites until not quite dry and fold into crumb mixture. With floured hands, roll the dough into small balls about the size of walnuts and drop into the simmering broth. Continue simmering uncovered, for 10 minutes. Sprinkle on chives and parsley and serve hot.

SCOTTISH HODGILS
(Border Broth Balls)

1 cup oatmeal
salt and pepper
broth skimmings
2 tablespoons chopped chives

Put the oatmeal into a bowl and add salt and pepper to taste. Add the fatty skimmings from the broth, enough to moisten the oatmeal and form a thick dough. Add the chives and blend well. Drop by tablespoons into simmering broth. Cook for 20 minutes and serve with meat from the soup.

RIVELS

1 egg, beaten
1 cup flour
1/2 teaspoon salt

Mix the egg, salt and flour thoroughly, then rub between the palms of the hands, letting the shreds drop on a clean cloth.

Cook in a pot of boiling broth or milk for 5 minutes.

FISH

Fish, unless preserved by one of a number of methods, is good only when very fresh. It lends itself to more methods and variations of preparation than almost any other type of food and, with the addition of eggs, vegetables, herbs, fruits and condiments, makes a complete diet. For those times when your fish comes fresh and sparkling from the water, with no fish merchant between to coddle it, it is wise to know how to handle the beast.

PREPARING FISH

• *Scaling* Briefly soak fish in lightly salted water and lay it on a board or other flat surface. Holding the tail firmly and using the back of a knife, scrape from tail toward head. Work quickly and be sure to remove all scales from the base of fins and head. Rinse under running water.

• *Cleaning* Slit the thin skin along the belly from the vent (tail opening) to the head;

remove and discard the entrails, but reserve the roe, for it is a great delicacy. Cut around the pelvic fins and remove them. Now cut off the head, including the pectoral fins, by cutting close above the collarbone and under the head bone; snap the bone by bending it over the edge of the board. Lastly cut off the tail. Now cut along both sides of the dorsal (back) fins and, pulling sharply and firmly toward the head, remove the fin with the root bone attached. Wash the fish under running water, removing blood and any remaining viscera and membranes. In some fish, such as herring, a black "skin" will be seen lining the stomach; rub it off with a damp towel or a little salt.

I have suggested discarding the entrails but nothing else, because the head, fin, tails and other bits of fish are invaluable in making the soup stock or Court Bouillon (see page 68).

• *For steaks*, simply cut slices crosswise, of the desired thickness.

• *To filet* is to cut away all bones; the fish may then be skinned or not. With a sharp knife, cut through the skin along the back from the tail almost to the head, then down the backbone. Twist the knife flat and, holding the skin taut, work from head to tail and lift the flesh from the back to the belly skin, running the knife as smoothly as possible over the rib bones. The entire side of the fish may then be lifted from the bones in one piece. Turn the fish over and repeat on the other side.

To skin the filets, lay them skin side down on the board. Hold the tail firmly and cut through the flesh to the skin. Turn knife flat under the flesh and push the knife forward, holding the free skin down.

• *To butterfly* fish is to filet it leaving the skin on and spreading the two sides, still held together by uncut flesh and skin.

• *Fat fish* are usually broiled, grilled, baked or steamed slowly and carefully. In this group are salmon, mackerel, herrings, pilchards, sardines, trout, carp and shad.

• *Lean fish*, being firm, are best fried, boiled or poached for the flesh will not fall apart as easily as fatter fish. Cod, flounder, sole, haddock and swordfish are lean.

• *Shellfish* are generally lean and are served in such a way to bring out their delicate flavors. Some larger types—lobster and large crab—are kept alive and plunged into boiling, salted water very briefly and either served immediately with melted butter or lemon butter or prepared according to a particular recipe.

• *Before using salt fish*, "freshen" by soaking in cold, fresh water overnight or for 12-16 hours. Change water from time to time and test for saltiness by pulling off a fin and tasting.

• If, during a sudden and unexpected cold spell, fresh fish has frozen (or if it is kept in a freezer), thawing it in a little cold milk will make it taste more like freshly caught fish than if it is slowly thawed at room temperature, when it often gets a dry, unpleasant flavor.

MEANS OF PRESERVING FISH

Salting down or pickling fish for long keeping are means as old as man himself. Any type of fish may be salted: flounder, sea bass, porgies, salmon, cod, haddock, herrings and sardines. The fish must be absolutely fresh to keep well. As soon as possible after being caught, remove entrails (and head and tail, if desired) and rinse in cold, running water. The backbone may then be removed and the fish cut into slices. Large fish such as cod are best beheaded and cut, but herrings and other small fish are generally left whole, or just cut along the backbone. Pack down in wide-mouthed, earthenware crocks, glass jars, a barrel or keg; the latter is considered best, for the brine that forms can then drip away.

SALTING DOWN

After thorough cleaning, many housekeepers simply rub the flesh with a generous amount of salt, inside and out, and pack the fish, strewing salt as they work. A few bay leaves, peppercorns or a handful of mixed whole pickling spices thinly distributed through the batch is nice. A big plate inverted over the top layer, weighted down with a clean rock, is necessary to keep fish from floating.

Alternately place one layer of salt on the bottom of the container and cover with a layer of fish; continue alternating layers of fish and salt until all fish are packed; finish with a heavy layer of salt. Leave in a cool, dry place for four days. Then, take out fish and wash under running water. Throw off the brine and clean the container thoroughly.

Make a saturated brine by pouring boiling water over salt (amounts depend on amount of fish to be cured), and add more salt until no more will dissolve. At that point, let the brine cool completely, then strain through double cheesecloth into the cleaned receptacle. Pack the fish in it, place a clean plate over the fish with a clean weight upon it to keep them below the surface of the brine. Cover with a clean cloth and leave for seven days. On the eighth day, remove the brine and discard. Again prepare saturated brine, cool and pour over the fish; they will keep until used.

It must be remembered that—as with all preserved foods—light and moisture must be avoided at all costs.

Examine the fish every day to be sure they are well covered with brine. If the odor becomes strong, drain immediately, rinse the fish under running cold water and cover with fresh brine. If this is done promptly the fish will not have a chance to spoil. Should you find it impossible to check for a few days and do eventually find an offensive odor, drain off the brine promptly and check to be sure there is no "foam" or yellowish matter present and that the fish is still firm to the touch. Should there be a suspicion of softness, throw them all away immediately!

Never mix fish of different varieties in the same container; each

fish has a distinctive odor and flavor and varies in the amount of fat; mixing them may kill all flavor.

CORNING

When refrigeration is unavailable, fish should be corned promptly; it will keep nicely up to 24 hours. When caught, bleed the fish by pulling out the gills completely and hanging the fish high, head down. As soon as possible, clean the fish (see page 61). Then mix table salt or coarse salt and pepper (about 1 cup salt to 1 tablespoon pepper) and use 2 tablespoons of this for every pound of fish. Rub into the intestinal cavity and over the outer skin. Put the fish into a basket or wooden box and wrap loosely. Before cooking, wash thoroughly.

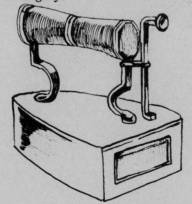

SMOKING

These procedures are also used preliminary to smoking. The one you select will be dictated by your situation and taste.

There are in general two methods for smoking fish: *hot smoking* and *cold smoking*. They may be used for any fish, but are particularly effective for fatty fish. Whether you use a smokehouse or a barrel, chips of hard, non-resinous wood such as apple, alder, oak, maple, hickory and locust are vital for long, slow smoking. Some woods impart a fragrance: juniper, rosemary, laurel and spicebush, for example. Green stalks are also good for starting, but must be washed or they may blacken the fish. Remember that the fire cannot be built up to last the night, but must remain constantly low and steady and never die out. *At no time must the fish get hot enough to cook or drip.*

HOT SMOKING

This prepares a fish so that it is partially or wholly cooked and will keep for only a very short period. The following directions are for a medium-size fish (about 8-12 pounds) at a medium cure; adjust to needs.

Split the fish down the back to one side of the backbone, so it will lie flat, yet in one piece, with the belly skin intact. If necessary with larger fish, cut out a section of the backbone just below the head. Scrape intestinal cavity, rinse thoroughly and place in a pail or bowl. Soak for 30 minutes in preliminary brine: dissolve 1/2 cup salt in a quart of water and pour over fish.

As the fish soaks, make a brine of:

2 pounds salt
2 cups sugar
1 teaspoon saltpeter
1 tablespoon peppercorns, crushed
6 bay leaves, crumbled
1 gallon water

Take the fish from the first brine and pack down in a keg, stoneware crock or large enamel kettle. (Do not pack in metal!) Pour on the second brine and let soak for about 3 hours, depending on the size of the fish, the amount of fat and how strong you like the flavor of the fish. (Remember this is a medium cure.)

Then rinse the fish under cold running water and hang outdoors in a cool, breezy place for about 3 hours; a thin, shiny skin will form on the surface.

Now put the fish in a smokehouse, about 3-4 feet from the source of smoke. Keep the fire very low and barely smoldering for the first 8 hours, during which the temperature should not exceed 90°. For the next 4 hours build up the smoke so it is very dense. Then increase the fire (or open the damper) to a temperature of 140° and cure at this temperature for 3 hours more or until the fish has a brown, glossy appearance. Remove from smokehouse and cool for 2-3 hours. A light coat of vegetable oil, brushed on gently while still warm, will improve the appearance of the fish. Wrap each fish in heavily-oiled paper (or waxed paper) and store in a cool dry place.

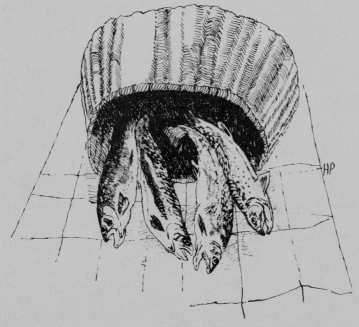

COLD SMOKING

Fish will keep much longer if the periods of brining and smoking are increased.

Clean fish promptly. The head may be removed but it is advisable to leave the hard bony section just below the gills, since it carries the weight during smoking. Split smaller fish down the back and spread out flat in one piece—keep belly skin intact. Larger fish may be cut in half lengthwise and backbone removed; then, if desired, cut in half again, lengthwise. This will facilitate handling. If the sides are not cut up, score them from head to tail with 1/4-inch incisions about 1 inch apart.

Wash fish thoroughly and soak for at least 30 minutes in a brine of 1 cup salt to 1 gallon water. Then wash brine off completely and drain well. If fish are small, pack each one into a wooden box, tub, keg or hardwood barrel containing fine salt, making sure the belly cavity is well coated. Sprinkle salt between each layer and cover completely. If fish are large, lay a 1/2-inch layer of salt on the bottom of the container. Lay fish skin side down on salt and alternate salt and fish until all are packed and salted. Last layer of fish should be skin side up and well covered with salt. Set a board or cloth over the top. Small fish should remain in the salt from 1-12 hours; large fish, from 1-3 days. Size, fatness and the length of time desired to keep the fish before using, determine the length of time of soaking. (Again, it is impossible to give exact figures; you will simply have to experiment.) A brine will form on the bottom of the container. It is best that it drain off, or be drained off. When finished, take the fish from the salt and rinse thoroughly. With a cloth, scrub off all salt and any waste that remains. Large fish may now go into the smokehouse. Small fish should be hung outdoors to dry, and if it is a still, hot day, fanned vigorously. Watch for the formation of a thin skin on the surface—in about 3-4 hours.

A couple of hours before the fish go into the smokehouse, start a low smoldering fire (see notes at beginning of this section). Since this is to be a long smoking, the heat should be low and the smoke not too dense during the first 8- to 12-hour period. Temperature should be about 80°, and no higher than 90°. If a thermometer is not handy, use your hand: if the air feels definitely warm, the temperature is too high.

Put small fish and fish pieces on a wire shelf along the wall; large fish should be hung about 8 feet away from the fire. After 8 to 12 hours, build up smoke until it is quite dense. Occasionally, turn the fish so all sides are evenly cured and have acquired a brown color. Small fish to be eaten within 2 weeks may be ready in 24 hours. Large fish, like salmon, might require 3-4 days and nights of even, steady smoking. Fish that are smoked for 5-6 days or more will keep up to 6 months. When ready, remove from smokehouse and wrap in paper. Hang in a dark, dry, cool place. Remember to examine often for mold. If it appears, remove it with a clean, dry cloth and resmoke the fish. Before using, freshen the fish by breaking or tearing into sections and soaking overnight in cold water. If still too salty, soak for an hour in milk, whole or skimmed.

SMOKING FISH
THE INDIAN WAY

This method is still used by the northwest Indians and is often done on beaches. It is generally used for medium-size fish like trout, salmon, pike, etc., and meant to prepare fish for immediate eating or for keeping no longer than 2-4 weeks.

Clean fish thoroughly and slit close to the backbone, from head *almost* to the tail. Make another cut along the other side of the backbone, exposing it. Break off the entire backbone, leaving no more than 1/5 of tail section uncut.

Spread the fish out flat, skin side up, and make long incisions about 1/4 inch deep and 1 inch apart on each side, like unconnected arrow marks. Wash fish well and wipe dry. Rub inside and out with a mixture of 1 tablespoon ground pepper to 2 cups salt. Set in a cool place overnight. In the morning, rinse each fish well.

Using 2 or 3 thin, flat sticks for each fish, attach by piercing fish crosswise to keep from curling. Hang them in an airy place until the surface moisture dries and a thin skin forms, about 3 hours. As soon as fish are hung, dig a shallow fire pit about 3-4 feet wide. Immediately start a fire so that when the fish are ready, gray embers will have formed. Use a good hard wood (maple, hickory, beech, alder or birch); old grape stakes and trunks are excellent.

Have ready long sticks about 4 feet in length, one for each fish. Split one end and put the fish within the split, so each side of wood holds it securely. Now thrust the free end of the long stick firmly into the ground at an angle, so the fish hang over the coals at a safe distance. Be sure they do not touch.

For smoking thoroughly (for long keeping), arrange 3 other longer sticks like a tripod or the frame of a teepee over the fish, with one end of each stick firmly thrust into the ground. Then lay thick layers of green boughs, grass and large leaves over the tripod, so the fish is enclosed, leaving only a hole in the covering, near the ground. (Through it the fire can be fed and controlled.) Place more green wood over the coals and build up a dense smoke, then cover the hole to keep the smoke in. From time to time, reach in and add more green wood to keep the smoke even. This must be kept up for 6-18 hours—the longer the cure, the longer the fish can be stored. When done, cool the fish, wrap and store in a dark, cool, dry place.

AIR DRYING

Another method, especially for cod, haddock or halibut, is to salt down thoroughly and after a few days, remove from keg and hang or lay fish over racks in the open air, to dry. When hard and dry as a board, these fish will keep almost indefinitely without refrigeration in a dark, cool, dry place.

BARREL SMOKEHOUSE

This method has been popular with small families and fishermen both in New England and on the West Coast. Usually, an old or discarded barrel is used, for it can never be utilized for other purposes again.

Obtain as large a barrel as possible and knock out both flat ends. Dig a hole or a pit in the ground about 2 to 3 feet deep and a little narrower than the diameter of the barrel. Place the barrel upright directly over the hole. Inside, a few inches below the top rim, nail two thin wooden strips opposite each other. Lay other sticks on top of these so that the ends will rest on the nailed-in strips. This second set of sticks must be removable; hang the fish on them and set in place; then lay board across the top of the barrel as a loose cover. Judge the direction of the prevailing winds and on the side from which the winds come, dig a "smokehouse pit": a hole about 2 feet deep, 2 feet wide and 12 feet from the hole in which the barrel sits. Connect the two pits by a covered trench. Arrange a cover for the fire pit—perhaps a sheet of metal—which will serve also as a damper, for when the lid is moved (a little or a lot) it admits air to build up or to "damp" the fire. Before smoking, prepare the fish and proceed as in other methods.

FISH

FISH STOCK
OR COURT BOUILLON

This is the basic stock in which to steam, poach or boil fish and may be used as the basis for fish sauces.

4 cups water
1 pound fish trimmings
   (head, bones, skin and tail)
1-1/2 tablespoons salt
1 onion
1 stalk celery
1 carrot
herb bouquet (parsley, celery
   leaf, leek, thyme, etc.)

Combine all ingredients in a pot, bring to a boil and simmer for an hour or more. Strain through double cheesecloth.

When boiled down to about 1/3 of the original quantity, this is called a "fumet."

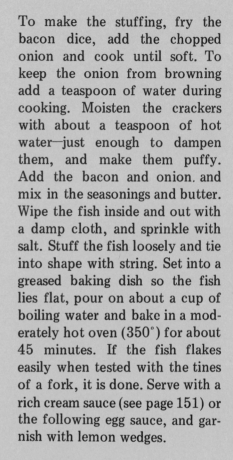

STUFFED BAKED SALMON

In 1796, Amelia Simmons, "the American Orphan," had this to say about salmon:

"Salmon . . . the noblest and richest fish taken in fresh water —the largest are the best. They are unlike almost every other fish, are ameliorated by being 3-4 days out of water, if kept from heat and the moon, which has much more injurious effect than the sun . . ."

1 whole salmon, 3-4 pounds
Stuffing
4 slices bacon, diced
1 large onion, chopped
2 cups crushed crackers
   (or cracker meal)
salt and pepper
pinch dried sage
sprig of thyme, crumbled
1 tablespoon butter, melted
1 cup boiling water
lemon wedges

To make the stuffing, fry the bacon dice, add the chopped onion and cook until soft. To keep the onion from browning add a teaspoon of water during cooking. Moisten the crackers with about a teaspoon of hot water—just enough to dampen them, and make them puffy. Add the bacon and onion. and mix in the seasonings and butter. Wipe the fish inside and out with a damp cloth, and sprinkle with salt. Stuff the fish loosely and tie into shape with string. Set into a greased baking dish so the fish lies flat, pour on about a cup of boiling water and bake in a moderately hot oven (350°) for about 45 minutes. If the fish flakes easily when tested with the tines of a fork, it is done. Serve with a rich cream sauce (see page 151) or the following egg sauce, and garnish with lemon wedges.

WHOLE POACHED SALMON WITH EGG SAUCE

This Yankee dish was carried to the West Coast and has remained a great favorite. It lends itself to varied treatment and may be simple or very elegant.

1 whole salmon, cleaned
Broth
1 large onion, thinly sliced
2 stalks celery with leaves, chopped
1 teaspoon salt
2 tablespoons vinegar
1/2 lemon, thinly sliced
1/2 teaspoon sugar
1 bay leaf
4 peppercorns
Egg Sauce
2 cups milk or light cream
1 small onion, sliced very fine
1 bay leaf
2 whole allspice
2 tablespoons butter
2 tablespoons flour
1 teaspoon salt
pinch pepper
2 hard-cooked eggs, mashed

If a French fish cooker with removable rack is not available, wrap the cleaned fish in a double thickness of cheesecloth, leaving long ends for easy handling. Tie the ends together securely. Select a kettle large enough to lay the fish flat, if possible.

To make the broth, spread all ingredients over the bottom of the kettle and pour in enough boiling water to barely cover the fish. Bring to a brisk rolling boil, then reduce the heat so it just barely simmers. Lift the fish by the cloth ends and lower gently into the kettle. Bring to a boil again, reduce heat promptly and simmer until the salmon is cooked (about 6 minutes to the pound). When it is ready, immediately grasp the cheesecloth ends, lift out the fish and put it on a large serving platter. To remove cheesecloth, lay the fish on the edge of the platter, grasp the end of the cloth and roll fish over gently to the center, pulling the cloth out from under the fish.

As the fish cooks, prepare the egg sauce. Heat the milk gently with the onion, bay leaf and all-spice, until a "skin" forms on the surface; skim it off. In another saucepan, melt the butter and stir in the flour until smooth, cooking briskly for a few minutes. Pour the scalded milk mixture into it gradually and, stirring constantly, cook over very low heat until the mixture bubbles. Remove from heat, season with salt and pepper and strain into another saucepan. Add the mashed eggs and heat through, but do not let it boil again. Serve in a sauceboat with the salmon. If the oily flavor of boiled salmon is objectionable to you, remove the skin and the dark flesh under it, before cooking.

THE SACRED COD

From the time the Pilgrims landed, codfish provided the main source of food in New England. The codfishing industry was well established as early as 1640 when, in one year, 300,000 codfish were dried for market.

New England fishermen called it sacred because they said it was the fish that Christ used to feed the multitude, for even today the marks of his thumb and forefinger are plainly to be seen on it. It is also said that the Devil stood by, watched the miracle and said he could do as well; he grabbed one of the fish with his hot fingers, but it slid out of his grasp, retaining for all time two long black scars on its sides. These stripes clearly differentiate the haddock from the cod. They are otherwise very similar even in taste and texture. Perhaps for this reason, haddock was not then in great demand; recently, however, it has grown in popularity.

Dried codfish (and haddock) were staples that could be carried well for long periods, even through heat. The Indians, of course, had used cod long before the white man came and they taught the early settlers how best to preserve it for winter use.

To begin with, use only the freshest fish. Remove the head, entrails and fins and wash the cod in a basin of salted water. Remove the backbone and either cut into 6-8 inch lengths or leave whole.

A hardwood barrel, a keg or a deep stoneware crock are the best containers. Before using, pour boiling water over the insides and dry quickly. Lay down a layer of coarse or rock salt about 1/2 inch thick, then a layer of fish covered with another layer of salt, and so on until all are used or the barrel is full. Set in a cool dark place for 4 days. Then remove the fish and wash in cold, running water for at least 20 minutes. Discard the old salt liquid, clean the container with boiling water and dry thoroughly. Make a saturated brine by pouring boiling water over salt and adding more salt until no more will dissolve. Cool completely and strain through cheesecloth.

Pack the fish in the container and pour on the brine. To prevent fish from floating, invert a clean dish over them and place a weight on it. The brine must cover the fish at all times. Set aside for 8 days, then repeat the process: drain off the old brine, discard, make a new saturated brine; rinse the container with boiling water, dry, pack down the fish, cover with cooled, strained brine and weight it well. Examine fish often, at least every 4 days. If a strong odor develops, drain, rinse, pack fish again in cleaned container and pour on strained, cooled brine.

When needed, remove the required amount of fish and "freshen" it in cold running water—or in several changes of water—overnight, then cook as desired.

COD SALAD

Traditionally served on St. Peter's Day, June 29th, a custom brought from the old country, where people living by the sea and making their living from fishing, made more of this day than people living inland. Obviously, it was St. Peter's connection with water and fish. The best fish of the day's catch was set aside and used for this dish.

1 codfish
3-1/2 to 4-1/2 cups water
1 teaspoon vinegar
1-1/2 teaspoons salt
3 cups water
1 chopped onion
1 stalk celery, chopped
1 bay leaf
3 peppercorns
1/2 teaspoon salt
cooked potatoes, sliced, or
    tiny new potatoes
mayonnaise
hard-cooked eggs, sliced
parsley and pickles for garnish

Make several diagonal slashes along the back of the fish about 2 inches long. Then marinate the fish in water to cover, with salt and vinegar added, for about 3 hours. Bring to a boil the additional 3 cups water, mixed with the onion, celery, bay leaf, peppercorns and salt; gently lay fish into the boiling stock; reduce heat and simmer for 10 minutes. Cool, drain and flake the fish. Spread a layer of the potatoes on a large platter and cover with flaked fish. Top with mayonnaise and garnish with eggs, parsley and pickles.

CODFISH PUDDING

1/2 pound dried codfish
1 tablespoon vinegar
3/4 cup raw rice
2-1/2 cups milk
2 tablespoons butter
2 eggs, well beaten
2 grinds fresh pepper
1/2 cup fine dry bread crumbs
butter
1/2 cup grated cheese (optional)

Soak the fish overnight, or for at least 12 hours, changing the water from time to time. Then drain, put into a saucepan and cover with boiling water. Add vinegar and cook very slowly until fish is tender. Drain, cool and remove the bones and skin. Flake the fish finely. Wash the rice in at least 6 changes of water and place in a heavy enamel saucepan (or top of double boiler) and add the milk. Cook gently for about 50 minutes or until liquid is absorbed and rice is just barely soft. Stir in the butter lightly with a fork. Add the flaked codfish, eggs and pepper and pour into a greased baking dish. Sprinkle on the bread crumbs and dot with bits of butter and the cheese, if used. Bake in a moderate (350°) oven until "set" and just barely browned (about 40 minutes).

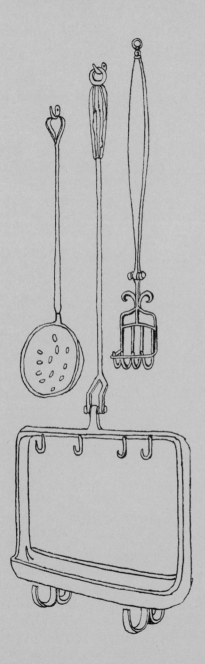

CODFISH CAKES

2 cups shredded dried codfish
3 medium potatoes
1 egg, well beaten
lard or butter for frying

A traditional New England dish, for breakfast or light supper, especially on Sundays.

Soak the dried codfish in cold water for about an hour. Squeeze out as much liquid as possible and put into a large saucepan with water to cover. Peel and quarter the potatoes and lay over the fish. Cook over moderate heat until the potatoes are just barely tender. Drain thoroughly then mash the potatoes and fish together as smoothly as possible. Stir in the egg and beat until fluffy. Drop by tablespoonfuls into deep, hot fat (375° on deep-fat thermometer). Cook until golden (4-5 minutes), remove with a slotted spoon and drain well. Serve with applesauce, fresh tomato sauce or green tomato pickles.

Note: Do not add salt.

HERRING

In early March of 1972, Point Richmond, California, had the heady experience of witnessing the "return of the herring," after ten years, to San Francisco Bay. Fish were taken avidly in nets— quite illegal, of course, yet even law officers stood around happily doing the same. The reasonable explanation was that what wasn't taken, the gulls would get and there they were, wheeling and diving and screaming and stealing herrings from each other. So greedy were the gulls that soon many couldn't even rise from the surface of the water, but foundered and beat their wings and screamed their protests to the laughing sun, and sat so low in the water they looked like over-loaded barges.

For me, it was a delightful experience. I was transported a century back to the days when the "run" must have been as welcome a sight to winter-hungry Californians as it was to New Englanders.

HERRING FORSCHPICE

Probably the most universally enjoyed herring dish is the simplest of all. Freshen the herring in water or milk for 24 hours, then rinse under cold running water and cut into serving pieces (fileted or not). Serve on toast or with boiled potatoes and a green salad. Garnish with wedges of hard-cooked eggs, chopped or thinly sliced onion and gherkins. Offer olive oil and vinegar in cruets for self serving.

HARINGSLA
(Pennsylvania Dutch
Mixed Herring Salad)

3 freshened herrings
1 small cooked beet, peeled
2 medium apples, cored,
    not peeled
1 medium onion, chopped fine
2 gherkins
8-10 cold cooked potatoes,
    peeled
1 hard-cooked egg, chopped
lettuce or other salad greens
2 tablespoons salad oil
1 tablespoon vinegar
salt and pepper to taste
mayonnaise
1 hard-cooked egg, sliced
lettuce

Bone the herrings and chop finely. Chop the beet and add the cored apple, onion, gherkins, potatoes and egg and chop until fine and smooth.
Shred the greens finely, pour all chopped ingredients into a large bowl and mix thoroughly. Pour on salad oil, vinegar, salt and pepper (the amount of salt to be used depends on how salty the herrings are). Arrange the salad in a mound on a large flat platter and smooth the surface with the back of a wet spoon. Coat with mayonnaise and decorate with slices of egg, small pieces of herring and bits of lettuce, if desired.

HADDOCK

Unlike cod, which is rarely smoked, haddock is often salted, smoked and even barbecued. *Finnan Haddie* is smoked haddock. Since it is lightly smoked, it requires refrigeration much like smoked salmon, and then it will keep very well for long periods. It may be prepared in a steamer or steamed in a saucepan, poached or boiled in milk or water and served with lots of sweet melted butter and boiled potatoes.

FLOUNDER

Flounder is one of the most delicate fish to be found in American waters; the European variety is sole.

SOUTHERN "SOLE" WITH ORANGES

4 tablespoons butter
6 filets of "sole"
    (or small whole flounders)
salt and pepper to taste
2 oranges
2 teaspoons lemon juice
2 tablespoons butter
1 teaspoon minced parsley
2 leaves minced fresh sage

Melt the butter in a large skillet and add the fish, turning so each piece is well buttered. Sprinkle with salt and pepper, cover tightly and cook over very low heat until fish flakes easily. Remove and keep warm while Peel and slice one orange to arrange around the fish.
Using the other orange, grate the peel into a saucepan and squeeze the juice over it. Add the lemon juice, butter and finely minced herbs. Stirring constantly, heat the sauce until it bubbles up and pour directly over the fish.

NEW ORLEANS
RED SNAPPER

1 3-4 pound red snapper
1 clove garlic, crushed
salt and freshly grated pepper
juice and grated rind
    of 1/2 lemon
1/2 teaspoon dried thyme
1 bay leaf
1 tablespoon olive oil
2 stalks celery with leaves,
    chopped
1/2 green pepper, chopped
3 tablespoons butter
1 medium onion, chopped
3 large tomatoes, diced
parsley

Scale and clean the fish and wash well. Pat dry and lay it in a shallow baking dish with lid. Mix together garlic, salt and pepper, lemon, thyme, bay leaf and olive oil and blend well. Rub this mixture into the fish, inside and out, cover and set in a cool place for 2 hours to marinate. Melt the butter in a heavy skillet and sauté the celery, pepper and onion in it until soft but not brown. Spread over the fish and add the tomatoes. Cover tightly and bake in a moderately hot oven (375°) for 3/4 hour. Baste once or twice with pan juices.

When fish flakes easily it is done. Carefully remove the fish to a warm serving platter.

Variation: Slice the red snapper and arrange slices in a deep baking dish. Just barely cover with water (or white wine), mixed with the juice of 2 limes or lemons, 2 chopped onions, 2 cloves crushed garlic, 2 hot peppers, chopped fine, and salt and pepper to taste. Put into a hot oven (425°) for about 20 minutes. Pour on 2 tablespoons of white vinegar and serve with boiled rice. Broiled bananas are a favorite accompaniment.

ROAST MOUNTAIN TROUT IN AN ENVELOPE

From a miner's memoirs, anonymous, 1848, we are given this method. "Fresh from the river, roll your trout in several layers of large green vine leaves (or wet paper) and roast it, like a potato, in the hot ashes of a camp fire." Be sure to pick leaves that will not give off a liquid or sap and be unpleasant to the taste.

DUTCH-STYLE EELS

This mode of preparing eel was very popular with the New Amsterdam Dutch and was soon learned by all New England. Use young eel and figure about 1/2 pound per serving, with another 1/2 pound "for the pot." Slice the eels into 2-inch pieces (after cleaning and skinning) and pack them upright and tightly together in a Dutch oven or high-sided skillet. Sprinkle on freshly ground black pepper, minced parsley and pour on vinegar or lemon juice. Leave the pan uncovered and simmer until all liquid evaporates. Be careful that the eels do not burn or dry out; add a little water if necessary.

This should take about 30 minutes. Serve them hot or cold with boiled potatoes or potato salad.

PENNSYLVANIA DUTCH SHAD ROE

The roe of shad is the most prized, but salmon, herring or roe of any fat fish is tasty.

roe
flour
salt and pepper
cornmeal
1 tablespoon bacon drippings
1 tablespoon butter

When cleaning the fish, take out the roe and set in a bowl of cold, salted water. Leave for no more than 5 minutes, then drop into boiling salted water for 5 minutes. Remove and drain well.
Dredge the roe with flour, salt and pepper and sprinkle on some cornmeal. Heat drippings and butter together and when it starts to foam, drop in the roe. Reduce heat immediately and fry gently to a golden brown, turning only once.
With a fork, test to be sure the roe is done throughout.

BAKED MULLET WITH FENNEL

This fish is found in southern waters and when small, is sometimes called the "sea woodcock," suggesting to connoisseurs that it may be eaten without eviscerating. It should, however, be rinsed thoroughly, scaled carefully and rinsed again.

1 mullet per person
salt and pepper to taste
2 tablespoons oil
1 small onion, chopped fine
2 tablespoons fresh minced
    fennel
bread crumbs
1 tablespoon lemon juice or
    fine white vinegar

Score mullet across the skin 2-3 times and sprinkle on salt and pepper. Heat the oil and sauté the onion until soft; stir in the fennel. Spread onion mixture on bottom of a baking dish and put the fish on it. Cover with a thin layer of bread crumbs and sprinkle on a little oil. Bake in a moderate oven (350°) for 25 minutes, then test with a sharp fork; if it flakes easily it is done. Remove from oven, sprinkle on lemon juice (or vinegar).

CATFISH

Catfish is rarely liked except by certain southerners, who have a passion for it. If taken from muddy water it should be kept alive in clean running water for a few days to rid it of the "mud" flavor; if from clear water, it is excellent immediately.

Catfish must be skinned (like eel and skate) for best results. In southern waters the blue catfish often reaches great size, especially in Louisiana. Traditionally, slices of catfish are deep fried and served with Hush Puppies.

DEEP FRIED CATFISH WITH HUSH PUPPIES

catfish
cracker or cornmeal
1 egg
1 tablespoon milk
lard for frying

Clean and skin the catfish then cut into thick slices. Dip slices into cracker or cornmeal then into a mixture of egg and milk and again into the crumbs or meal. The traditional southern fat is lard, but a vegetable oil may be used, if preferred. The fat must be very hot. Put the coated fish into a frying basket, immerse in the fat and cook until golden brown (do not crowd the fish; kettle should be large and roomy). Serve at once with Hush Puppies fried in the same fat as the fish.

HUSH PUPPIES

3 cups boiling water
1-1/2 cups cornmeal
1 teaspoon salt
1 large onion, chopped fine
deep fat for frying

Very slowly, add the cornmeal to the boiling water, stirring constantly with a wooden spoon; be sure the cornmeal does not "lump." Add the onion and keep cooking until very smooth and slightly thickened. Drop by spoonfuls (the same wooden spoon) into the very hot fat (after fish are fried in it) and turn them from time to time. Remove when nicely browned on both sides.

ABALONE

Long before the white man came, the Indians used abalone for food and the shells for decoration. At that time, they were abundant and easily obtainable at low tide. The abalone is very slow growing; the female is 6 years old before she can spawn. Therefore, the early voracious gathering of them soon depleted the supply and they are now protected by law. The prettiest and best—the Pink Abalone—is found off British Columbia and Alaska. Only about 4-5 inches in diameter at its largest, it is so tender that it needs little pounding, unlike the larger kinds to the south. Those along the California coast are found on the underside of rock ledges where they are quite hidden and must be probed for carefully. Slip a long steel bar under the shell very quickly and pry it off before the abalone takes a tighter grip. It is very dangerous to try to take it with the hands, for if you put your fingers under the shell, a large abalone can grasp them firmly and hold you down long enough to endanger you.

To clean abalone, remove the muscle from the shell and cut away the large green viscera, which is not edible. Slice the muscle horizontally into thin slices, between a 1/4 and a 1/2 inch thick; then, with a wooden mallet, steak tenderizer or a bottle, pound each slice thoroughly.

To cook, first dip each steak into an egg beaten with a little water, then dip into seasoned flour or cracker crumbs. Fry in hot butter, bacon drippings or oil. Cook rapidly and only until just done, for best flavor.

ABALONE AND EGG

My favorite method, however, is to dip the steak into a thin batter made of 2 eggs beaten with a teaspoon each of flour and oil, and some salt and pepper. Drop the steak into very hot fat and cook 1 minute; then turn, cook 1 more minute and serve. It should look like soft scrambled egg and taste like heaven!

SQUID

To clean squid, prepare a bowl of cold water with a tablespoon of vinegar or lemon in it. Cut off the tentacles just above the eyes. Grasp the head and pull firmly, so all the innards come out in one piece. Then, feel around the body for the "bone"—actually a cartilage the length of the body or *mantle*, as it is called—and pinch the end of it and pull out. Discard "bone" and innards and toss tentacles and mantle into the acidulated water. How the mantle is then treated depends entirely on the recipe used. For stuffed squid, it is left whole, of course. For frying Japanese style, cut the length of the mantle and lay it flat; cut into large squares about 2 inches square (or longer and narrower) and score it criss-cross with a sharp knife so the pieces will curl up in heat. Chinese style is to cut into 1-inch squares. Italian style is, usually, to cut slices about 1/2 inch wide. Otherwise, for chowders and stews, chop fine or coarse, as desired. It is important to remember that overcooking toughens this flesh.

CARP

Carp is a fresh-water fish, and like mackerel and similar fat fish is best boiled, baked, broiled or pickled with vegetables and spices. When fried, vinegar or lemon juice should be used generously. After cooking, drain fish well.

PICKLED CARP

carp
onions, thinly sliced
lemons, thinly sliced (optional)
4-5 cloves
1 teaspoon mustard seed
1 gallon vinegar
1 cup brown sugar
1/2 cup salt

Pickled carp or mackerel was much used on the inland frontiers for it kept well and made a nice light supper.

Clean and scale the fish. Cut down the backbone and separate the two sides. Soak in milk overnight and drain well.

Put a layer of fish, skin side down on the bottom of a crock (or glass jar). Mix together the onions, lemons, cloves and mustard seed and lay a thin layer on the fish. Cover with another layer of fish, then of spice and so on until all fish are used.

Dissolve the sugar and salt in the vinegar and pour over the fish until well covered. Press with a plate and clean weight, then cover with a cloth; let stand in a cool, dry, dark place for at least 10 days before using. It will keep well for months.

CLAMBAKE

Of all the gifts the Indian gave the white man, those who live near the sea believe that the greatest was the clambake. Although it has been added to, elaborated and often "fancified," in essence it has not been improved upon. Basically, clams, fish, lobsters, corn, chickens and so on are cooked in the steam from rockweed spread over hot stones, and all is covered over to keep in the steam and flavors.

The clambake became the favorite kind of large party in New England; politicians were introduced to their constituents there, churches held annual outings in this way, and lodges, societies and public and private parties were so celebrated; and each section of New England has its very own preferences dating back to the earliest days.

While some gather the seafood, others prepare the fire, burning big pieces of hard wood on a thick layer of large stones, until the stones are white hot. Brush off embers and put a thick layer of seaweed on the hot stones. Put down the clams and spread another layer of seaweed. Potatoes in their jackets—both white and sweet—may be put down, with a layer of husked corn on top, covered with the husks. Pieces of fish and sausages wrapped in cheesecloth or muslin are laid over the corn husks; chickens cover that and lobsters on the very top. Then throw a heavy wet canvas, or a large blanket, in the Indian fashion, over the whole pile and keep it wet during the baking; hold down the edges with rocks and seaweed. The steam from the clams and the seaweed seems to tenderize and flavor every other ingredient during the 45 minutes or an hour it takes to penetrate the layers and cook everything thoroughly.

On a side table put the makings for salad, and condiments such as salt, pepper, hot pepper sauce, sliced raw onions, sliced tomatoes, pitchers of melted butter, vinegar, lemon wedges and piles and piles of bread of every kind: brown, white, corn, whole wheat.

When the covering is lifted, move aside each layer until the clams are exposed. They are eaten first: spread shells apart (saving the clam juice in a cup provided for the purpose), lift clams out and dip into hot, melted butter. Only then are the other ingredients of the clambake eaten.

OYSTERS

The Creole cooks used oysters in as many ways as people in other areas and dreamed up a few new recipes as well. One of the most original recipes for their use is so delicious it came to be known all over the South, with variations, of course. It was *La Médiatrice* (the peacemaker) so called for its alleged origin in New Orleans. Gentlemen who, after staying out into the wee hours without their wives and expecting an irate reception at home, would stop en route and purchase long loaves of French bread, which were cut lengthwise and filled with lightly sautéed oysters. The "lid of the coffin," as it was called, was then replaced and the steaming hot delicacy carried home. What wife could resist or be angry?

LOBSTER

The lobster of the cold Atlantic waters is the only true lobster in American waters. The "lobster" found in the Pacific is a form of crayfish, closer to the *langouste* of France. True lobsters have great meaty claws, the others have small claws and are, in fact, smaller animals. There is a third type from the South African cape, the tails of which are found in American market freezers.

BOILED LOBSTERS

The most delicious way to prepare the Atlantic lobster is simply to boil it. The lobster must be alive at time of cooking: a fresh live lobster will curl its tail under its body when it is picked up. They are dark blue-green and, after cooking, turn bright "lobster red."

For 6 lobsters boil several gallons of water and add 3 tablespoons of salt and any preferred herbs. Bring to a brisk rolling boil and plunge in the lobsters. Cover kettle, bring back to a boil, reduce heat and simmer for 20 minutes. Lift out lobsters, drain and serve with melted butter and lemon wedges.

To remove lobster meat from cooked lobster, cut through the thick membrane on the underside of the shell; peel back with one hand and pull meat toward you with the other.

SHRIMP DE JONGHE

A Dutch dish, this was very popular for dinner parties in New Amsterdam.

1 cup dry bread crumbs
1/4 pound butter
1/2 cup dry white wine
2 tablespoons minced
   green onions
1 clove garlic, mashed
1/2 teaspoon each fresh tarragon,
   chervil and minced parsley
1/4 teaspoon fresh thyme
pinch cayenne
1 teaspoon salt
freshly ground black pepper
1 pound freshly cooked
   shrimp, peeled
cold butter and minced chervil

Mix and blend all ingredients except the shrimp. In a well-buttered baking dish—or 6 individual baking dishes—put down a layer of the bread crumb herb mixture and top with a layer of shrimp; continue alternating layers to the top, ending with a layer of bread crumbs. Dot with bits of cold butter and a light sprinkling of chervil. Bake in a hot oven (400°) for 20 minutes.

Serve with the same dry white wine used in it.

MUSSELS

STEAMED MUSSELS
(or Clams)

Be sure the mussel (or clam) has tightly closed shells; if even slightly open, reject it like the plague. Between its lovely blue shells, the mussel grows a "beard" called the byssus, with which it attaches itself to ropes, rocks or whatever. Grasp this beard firmly and pull off. Then scrub the shells thoroughly and briskly, with brush or pot scrubber.

If it is meant to be the main dish of the meal, figure about a dozen or a dozen and a half per person, if for a snack or appetizer figure about a half dozen for each person. This recipe is for a main dish for 6 persons, with 18 mussels for each.

9 dozen mussels
3/4 cup water or dry white wine
herb bouquet: parsley, thyme,
   celery stalk and leaves
1 tablespoon olive oil or butter
lemon butter for dunking

Put the mussels in the largest kettle you own. Pour on the water or wine, the herb bouquet (either tied together or finely minced, as desired) and over all, the olive oil. Cover tightly and start with high heat; when it bubbles, turn heat down and steam until all the shells are open, 15-20 minutes. Immediately remove the mussels to a large bowl and strain the juice into a pitcher or saucepan. As each person helps himself to mussels, he should pour some of the broth over them. A small cup of lemon butter for each person should be made available.

HARD-SHELLED CRABS
(East or West Coast)

Even in small towns along the coastline, crabs can be bought—in season—raw or cooked, at any local market.

HOW TO CLEAN A CRAB AFTER COOKING

Turn crab on its back and break off the "fingers" on underside of body. Turn over, grasp shell at the rear, off center, with one hand and the body with the other, and firmly pull upward; the shell should come off in one piece. Scoop out and save the crab "butter." (Though many do not like it, it has subtle flavor and is wonderful to add to a sauce.) Remove and discard all soft matter in the shell, including the feathery, grayish gills. Wash under running cold water. Break the crab shell in half along the center line or keep intact and serve crab salad or deviled crab in it. Pull off the legs and claws and crack them with a hammer, or serve whole with nutcrackers.

To prepare boiled crab see directions on boiling lobsters (page 80). A nice way to serve boiled crab is to wash the shell clean, fill it with parsley and lay crabmeat on top. Surround with claws and serve on a bed of crushed ice.

GAME, GAME BIRDS AND POULTRY

"My fare is really sumptous this evening: buffaloe's humps, tongues and marrow-bones, fine trout, parched meal, pepper and salt and a good appetite; the last is not considered the least of the luxuries."
Journals of Lewis and Clark, 1805

The frontier. can sometimes be found in such unlikely places as smack in the middle of New York City. During World War II, we lived in an old brownstone, where many of our friends in the service spent their leaves with us. Meat was severely rationed and it was some time before we discovered that we could buy all kinds of unrationed gamé at the great Washington Market and at the public market in Harlem. Buffalo, elk, venison, boar, pheasant, partridge, 'possum, coon, geese, ducks, hare, rabbit, wild turkey and so on, all properly aged and ready to cook. It was not cheap, of course, but it was available. My notes and recipes of the time demonstrate how far one can stretch three pounds of buffalo, venison, a brace of pheasant or duck if one had to. Comparing those notes to recorded frontier game recipes, I find not too much difference, though I've often wondered how alike were the final flavors.

Marinades are a most important part of game cookery, since so much of it is either strongly flavored or tough textured. Buffalo, for example, benefitted greatly by being marinated. I admit to making marinades of whatever was at hand, and to using them over and over again as long as they lasted. My herbs were mainly dried, but I bought small amounts. What fresh ones I could grow I washed very thoroughly; Rockefeller Center dropped soot like black snow on my tender greens.

During colonial times game was amazingly abundant, according to letters of European visitors traveling through the East. By the mid-1700's, however, accounts show that game was getting very scarce. Buffalo had moved westward and were rarely seen; where game had, only a few years earlier, been shot from the cabin door, it had now virtually disappeared except for small animals. To have game to salt, dry, pickle and smoke for the winter, hunters went great distances and were gone for months at a time. They went out with large supplies of cornmeal, salt, flour, red pepper, ham and "jerk," both plain and pounded into pemmican (mixed with fat, maple syrup or sweet dried berries or molasses ; see page 84).

A favorite dish of these "long hunters" was a stew consisting of the choicest bits of big wild game put into a kettle, with or without seasoning, and cooked, sometimes overnight, until the aroma drove them to digging into it. The stew was, much later during the Gold Rush, dubbed, "son-of-a-bitch " stew. It was a precursor of the favorite dish of the western range: the chuck wagon of the American cowboy.

VENISON

If the animal is young, the meat can be used without tenderizing or aging. If older, marinating will tenderize it and substitute for the "hanging" period once resorted to; it will also help to overcome the "gamey" taste to which some object.

JERKY

Jerky may be made out in the sun, over a fire or in an oven at home, as long as the heat is kept very very low, so it is dried rather than cooked. An oven 160-175° is about right; I always prefer to keep the oven door slightly open so all moisture can escape. Simply trim the fat from the meat and cut it into strips about 1/8th inch thick, long or short as you prefer. It may be sprinkled with some pepper but salt only adds moisture, I believe. Lay the meat on wire racks—or on cheesecloth over a rack—in a baking pan. Put the meat into a preheated oven and leave until it is quite dessicated: crisp and stiff. If there is any doubt that the "jerk" is done, turn off heat and leave the meat in overnight. About 3-5 pounds of fresh meat will usually yield about a pound of jerky. Put into jars or crocks and keep airtight until wanted. Note: Brushing oven-dried meat with liquid smoke gives it an outdoor touch. In the Southwest, some salt and coarsely ground hot chili peppers are rubbed into meat before drying. Jerky may be made of any meat.

PEMMICAN

Pemmican is so concentrated a food that it was a staple among the Plains Indians, particularly for use on long journeys. Leather pouches were made to carry it. A Blackfoot pouch is made of the 4 legs and feet of a deer. The skin is split up the back and spread wide, then all 8 sides are sewn together edge to edge into a square pouch with a foot at each corner (to stand on, of course). The top "circle" of leather is pulled together with a thong to make a delightful purse. These are called, in fact, "pemmican bags."

Jerky is pounded in a mortar until it is powder dry. Melted fat (of the bear preferably) and dried berries or maple syrup are then pounded into it to make a sweet paste. As the fat cools, it becomes a solid mass. A more concentrated source of pure energy cannot be imagined nor a more easily carried form of nourishment. The old recipes called for 50 pounds meat, 40 pounds fat, 5 pounds berries (dried) or more to taste. They often altered the flavor by using 2 different fats.

VENISON AND BEANS CASEROLE

This recipe was given to Betty Pearson by Peggy Cartright and used by all in the "settlement" of Point Richmond, California.

1 pound dried red kidney beans
6 cups cold water
salt and pepper
1/2 pound sausages, sliced
1 pound boneless venison
   (or more)
2 onions, chopped
2 cloves garlic, minced
1/2 teaspoon dried rosemary
   or oregano
3/4 cup dry red wine or broth
2 teaspoons salt
pepper
dash cayenne

Soak kidney beans overnight. Discard liquid and pour beans into a large kettle; pour on 6 cups water and salt and pepper and cook gently until tender. In a large casserole, mix the cooked beans with the remaining ingredients, cover and bake in a moderate oven (350°) for 1-1/2 hours. Note: If desired, the meat, onions and sausages may be browned in 2 tablespoons fat, before mixing with other ingredients.

VENISON MULLIGATAWNEY STEW

This modified version of Mulligatawney Stew is the gift of Monica Haley, good neighbor and wife of John Haley, painter, sculptor, builder and hunter.

4 pounds venison roast
4 tablespoons salad oil
1 onion, chopped
16 carrots cut in 2-inch chunks
16 stalks celery, cut in
   2-inch chunks
1 teaspoon salt
2 apples, diced
2 cups beef broth
1 tablespoon chopped parsley

Cut the meat into strips or cubes. Heat the oil in a heavy Dutch oven and brown the meat well; add the onions and cook over moderate heat until tender. Add the carrots, celery, salt, apples and beef broth and bake in a moderate oven for 2 hours. Sprinkle on the parsley, cook 10 minutes more and serve hot.

VENISON SIGNORA CARA

2 cups red wine vinegar
2 cups white wine
3 cloves garlic, crushed
2 tablespoons chopped parsley
2 whole cloves
1 large onion, chopped
4 pounds venison
   (rack, loin or leg)
salt and pepper
3 tablespoons flour
4 slices salt pork
1 medium onion, sliced
1 cup water

Combine vinegar and wine in a saucepan and bring to a boil; remove from heat, add garlic, parsley, cloves and onion; stir and cool.
Place the venison in a glass or porcelain wide, shallow bowl and pour the marinade over it. Let stand overnight (or a full day), turning occasionally. Then, remove meat and pat dry.
Sprinkle with salt and pepper, rub with flour and put into a large baking pan; cover with salt pork and onion slices. Brown in a very hot oven (450° or more), then add 1 cup of the marinade, reduce heat to 350° and roast for about 2 hours, or until tender, adding more marinade, if needed.

SON-OF-A-BITCH STEW

This was an ingenious source of quick energy, serving as food and drink to men isolated in the wilderness. At the start it was made with buffalo, deer, moose, bear, or elk innards, and perhaps a beaver tail, which was valued for its fat. Most of these animals were herbivorous so their "inwards" were sweet and tender.

The initial preparations were simple and direct: after bleeding, the animal was slit, belly side, from chin to tail, the liver removed promptly and often immediately impaled on a stick, cooked over the fire and devoured. Then into the great kettle went the kidneys, heart, brains, udder, intestines, among other parts and, finally, certain "unnameable parts," if the beast was male. Particularly favored was the "marrow gut" (the tube connecting the two stomachs of cud-chewing animals) from young animals, for it held undigested milk, a substance much like marrow. Perhaps a handful of hot peppers was thrown in if available. At the very end, a pint of rum might be added, but no water, no vegetables, no herbs.

Natural juices escaped and made up the gravy and the whole was simmered and simmered until hunting knives were plunged in and chunks were stabbed and eaten. If someone had a bit of flour, it was mixed with water and maybe a wild egg, made up into biscuits that floated on the top until cooked, somewhat like dumplings. Or a hole was dug in a hillside, a fire built and, in the resulting embers, the bread was baked. What more could anyone ask?

BEAR

The bear was taken for his pelt as well as for food. The meat was believed to "increase a man's potency" and the foot was the preferred part, but, it is said, looked too much like a human foot for some delicate English tastes. The animal was skinned immediately after the kill and the liver eaten promptly (not unlike all wild animals). The meat was then cut up and carried home in the pelt. The fat was, if at all possible, rendered and clarified (with shavings of slippery elm bark which would "keep it fresh for future use") and carried in the emptied bladder. At home, the tongue, sides and ribs were treated like pork: salt-cured and smoked. The pelt, when treated properly, was soft and warm; it was cherished as a rug or bed cover and served for legal tender in many trading posts.

BRAISED BEAR

4-5 pound slice of bear loin
1 teaspoon salt
3 crushed peppercorns
1 bay leaf, crumbled
1 cup vinegar
1/2 cup water
1/2 cup vegetable oil or butter

Lay meat in a wide and shallow bowl and pour remaining ingredients, well blended, over it. Turn meat several times and keep in a cool place for about 2 days.

When ready to use, wipe the meat with a damp cloth and cut it into 1-1/2-inch slices. Place in a heavy skillet over very high heat. Dust with salt and pepper and, when meat is well seared, turn it over. Brush uncooked side with butter and sprinkle on 1 tablespoon of marinade. After a few minutes, reduce heat and cook until done. Add more of the marinade as needed.

BOAR

The Spanish called the small boar a *javelina*, their name for wild sows or boars. It is also sometimes called *peccary*. The best way to prepare a young boar, is to treat it like Roast Suckling Pig (see page 104). It should be no more than 16-18 pounds. Be sure to remove all bristles before cooking—immediately after killing is the best time. Rub all surfaces, inside and out, with salt, pepper and some fat or oil. Truss well. After spitting, place over the fire far enough away so the skin does not crack or blister and baste very often with butter or oil, to which 3 or 4 cloves of chopped garlic are added. Turn back to the fire first, and when quite hot but not yet seared, turn over, and keep turning fre-

quently. It should take about 3 hours to cook thoroughly; the meat should come easily from the bones before the inside parts are done.

Before skewering, some like to fill the stomach cavity with a few apples; core them and fill with currants, if desired. A very nice basting brush is made with branches of thyme, rosemary, oregano or savory, dipped into the basting liquid.

The flesh may also be cured: salted, smoked or preserved in brine like any part of the pig.

WILD GOAT

If a young animal, it may be treated like the boar, pig or very young lamb; if small enough, spitted and roasted whole or in the oven.

MOUNTAIN GOAT STEW

3 pounds goat meat, without bones
1/2 cup flour (corn, millet or wheat)
1 teaspoon salt
1/4 teaspoon black pepper
1/2 teaspoon dried sage
1/2 teaspoon dried thyme
1 teaspoon dried marjoram
2 teaspoons dried parsley
3 slices salt pork
2 medium onions
1 large carrot, sliced
1 small turnip, sliced
8 potatoes, peeled and quartered

For this recipe one may use the tougher cuts of goat meat such as the brisket, neck, rump or chuck. Cut out the bones and fat, but do not discard. Wash and dry the meat and cut it into 2-inch cubes. Combine flour, salt, pepper and herbs and dredge the meat in the mixture. Fry the salt pork in a heavy Dutch oven; then brown the meat well in the pork fat. Add enough water to barely cover and simmer for 2 hours. Add the vegetables and simmer for 1 hour longer. Twenty minutes before serving, add biscuits or drop dumplings (made of sourdough, cornmeal or wheat flour). Cover tightly and cook over medium heat.

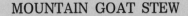

BUFFALO

"...we cut our juicy buffalo meat into thin strips and hung it on the bushes to dry. It took 2 whole days to dry it completely. ... Then we packed the meat into the back of the wagon. As it was completely dry, we did not have to worry about whether it might spoil on us."

Heinrich Leinhard's diary
"From St. Louis to
Sutter's Fort, 1846"

Newcomers (called "greenhorns") would often be stricken with what was called *mal de vache* after the first taste of buffalo meat; diarrhea and fever was the result. However, they became so inured to it afterward that they could eat many pounds daily with the broth. So dependent on it did many travelers become that thirsty men even drank the liquid in the paunch of the freshly killed buffalo.

There is little chance even ambitious hunters are likely to kill a buffalo today, though the government-protected herds are, in certain seasons, thinned out so the pasturage will suffice. The slain animals are then sold off to connoisseurs, who apply early for the meat by writing to such places as Custer State Park, Hermosa, South Dakota.

Buffalo meat may be prepared much like tough beef. Marinating helps to tenderize and cut cooking time; use the marinade as the needed liquid and cook very slowly.

SMALL GAME

While large game like bear, even deer and antelope are still to be hunted (though one's catch must be limited in many ways)—small game such as rabbit, squirrel, badger, coon, groundhog, woodchuck and so on, still may be freely taken in many parts of the country.

HASENPFEFFER

2 4-pound rabbits
1-1/2 cups dry red wine
1/2 cup vinegar
1 medium onion, minced
1 tablespoon mixed whole
   pickling spice
2 teaspoons salt
1/2 teaspoon freshly ground
   pepper
flour, salt and pepper,
   mixed for dredging
4 slices salt pork, diced large
2 tablespoons butter
1 large onion, sliced thin
2 cloves garlic, mashed
2 tablespoons brown sugar
1 cup chicken stock
1 tablespoon lemon juice
1/2 cup sour cream

Cut each rabbit into 8 serving pieces. In a large glass or pottery bowl, mix the wine, vinegar, onion, pickling spices, salt and pepper; marinate the rabbit pieces in this mixture in a cool place, turning often, for at least 2 days. Remove rabbits, pat dry and dredge with the flour, salt and pepper mixture.

In a very heavy flameproof casserole (or Dutch oven) fry the salt pork mixed with butter until pieces are crisp; then remove hard bits and reserve. Brown the pieces of rabbit in the resulting fat, turning often; when browned, remove and keep warm. Brown the onion and garlic in the same pan, stir in the sugar and cook for 3 minutes. Pour off most of the fat in the pan and add to remaining fat 1 cup of the marinade and 1 cup chicken or veal stock. Return rabbit to the pan and bring liquid to a brisk boil; reduce heat, cover tightly and simmer for about 1-1/2 hours, adding more marinade if needed. The liquid should just barely cover the meat at all times. The rabbit may also be baked in a moderately slow oven (325°). Meat should be very tender when done. Return the salt pork bits to the pan and stir in the lemon juice and sour cream.

LOUISIANA CREOLE RABBIT

2 or 3 pound young rabbit
1/4 cup milk
1/2 cup flour
1-1/2 teaspoons salt
1/4 teaspoon freshly ground
   pepper
3 tablespoons butter or oil
Creole Sauce (see below)

Cut the rabbit into serving pieces and dip in milk, then roll in a mixture of the flour, salt and pepper. Heat the fat in a heavy skillet and brown the rabbit lightly. Then make the sauce as the rabbit simmers:

CREOLE SAUCE

3 tablespoons butter or oil
2 medium onions, sliced thinly
1 clove garlic, mashed
3-1/2 cups tomato juice

Heat the fat and sauté the onions and garlic until golden. Add tomato juice and bring to a boil; reduce heat and simmer for 15-20 minutes.

Pour sauce over the rabbit, cover pan tightly and bake in a moderately hot oven (325°) for 1-1/2 hours. Uncover pan and bake 1/2 hour longer.

HARE LOAF

1 large hare (or 2 small ones) to
    make about 7-8 pounds
    before dressing
pork (same weight as dressed,
    boned hare)
mild vinegar
1 medium onion (or leek or
    wild onions)
1 stalk celery with leaves
    and root
1 tablespoon fresh savory
1 tablespoon minced parsley
salt and pepper
2 eggs
1 bay leaf
1 teaspoon fresh thyme leaves
bacon, sliced very thin
bones of the hare
1 veal or pork knuckle
1 calf's or pig's foot
1/2 tablespoon salt
1 egg white

Skin the hare, cut it open, reserve the liver and clean inside and out thoroughly. Then bone it: with a sharp knife, make long incisions along the leg bones and cut away the flesh. Cut along the bone structure of the loins and take meat off in pieces as large as possible. Reserve bones.

In a large, shallow bowl, cover pieces of hare meat with very mild vinegar (if strong, dilute). Set aside in a cool place for 12 hours. Then cut the meat in very thin slices.

Grind together twice the hare's liver and the pork, add the onion, celery, savory, parsley, salt, pepper and whole eggs. Blend thoroughly. Spread mixture over the bottom and sides of a large casserole or tureen. Neatly arrange the slices of hare and top with a layer of the pork mixture. Sprinkle with crumbled bay leaf and thyme and cover with thin slices of bacon or pork lard. Cover the casserole very tightly (if lid is not tight, fill edges with flour-and-water paste). Set in a pan of hot water and put into a preheated oven (300°) for at least 2-1/2 hours. As this bakes, cook the broth:

Put hare bones, veal knuckle and calf's foot into a large soup kettle. Cover with water, add salt and simmer for 2-1/2 hours.

When the loaf is done, remove the lid and cover with a dish, inverted to fit tightly over the meat; put a weight on the dish to press out all excess juices. Add these to the broth.

Raise heat under the broth and let boil to reduce it a little.

Beat the egg white and add to the broth to clarify it. Strain through double thickness of muslin and pour over the loaf, to cover. Let cool thoroughly.

Variation: Substitute brandy or dry, red wine for the vinegar, for a more subtle and interesting flavor.

If calf's foot and knuckle are not available, make a very thick gelatin, using the liquor pressed from the loaf for the liquid, plus a very little white wine. (Follow directions on unflavored gelatin package but use 3/4 of the liquid requirement.)

BRUNSWICK STEW

In our southland, Brunswick Stew came to be associated with Election Day rallies and was made in vast amounts. There are many versions of it, since it is that kind of a dish; a little of this, that and whatever one cares to add or take away.

2 cups dried lima beans
2 squirrels, skinned and cleaned
flour, salt and pepper
1/2 pound diced bacon
1 ham bone with some meat
    left on
2 onions, sliced
2 stalks celery with leaves,
    chopped
2 cups whole kernel corn
4 cups skinned, cut-up tomatoes
1 cup sliced okra
6 potatoes, peeled and boiled
1 pod red pepper, crushed
1 tablespoon sugar
herb bouquet: bay leaf, parsley
    thyme, savory, tied together

Soak the beans overnight. Cut the cleaned squirrels into serving pieces, and dredge with flour, salt and pepper. In a large skillet, fry the bacon and when crisp remove the hard bits. Brown the squirrel in the bacon fat. Place ham bone in a large Dutch oven and put browned pieces of squirrel over it. Add the beans, the bacon bits, onions and celery and cover with boiling water; cover tightly and simmer for 2 hours. Then add remaining ingredients and simmer for another hour. Mix a little flour with water and stir into the stew to thicken it. Cook briskly for 5 minutes. Taste to correct seasoning and serve.

Brunswick Stew often had veal added to it, chickens, ham, even beef; sometimes it was made with a few rabbits, sometimes with a few chickens.

GAME BIRDS

Squabs, blackbirds, thrushes, rails, warblers, doves, larks, snipes, woodcocks and all other small birds that eat only insects and berries are quite clean, and thus are often plucked but not drawn before cooking. That is to say, they are cooked with their innards, though the giblets may be removed for gravy. Usually, they are simply salted and peppered and broiled, whole. Melted butter may be brushed on during broiling and they are turned often.

They are delicious served over cornmeal mush (or polenta) with melted butter poured on. Salt, pepper and herbs are sprinkled over before serving.

SMOKED BIRDS

Smoked birds can be eaten without further cooking, but can also be steamed, baked or fried. They should always be washed thoroughly and wiped dry before preparing. If making a stuffing, omit salt, for the juices of the bird will provide enough salt during cooking. Bake, uncovered, in a very slow oven (about 250-275°) and

turn often. Do not use the pan drippings for basting; they will be too strong in flavor. Instead combine a little vinegar diluted in water with some mustard, powdered cloves and brown sugar. If the bird is rather old and very large, it may be better to steam it slowly.

BROILED YOUNG GAME BIRDS

Clean the birds and chop the giblets. Split birds down the backs and spread wide; flatten with a mallet or cleaver. In a baking dish, place each bird on a thick piece of bread. Cover each with 2 slices of bacon and sprinkle the chopped giblets over them. Top with a small pat of butter and bake in a very hot oven (425-450°) for 30-40 minutes. Watch that they do not burn. Baste with a little wine, water or chicken stock from time to time.

FRIED GAME BIRDS

Clean birds thoroughly, split them down the back and spread open. Rub all surfaces with onion or garlic, salt and pepper. In a heavy skillet brown the birds in butter or bacon fat. Add a little red wine or stock or water, cover tightly and steam over medium heat until tender. Make a gravy of the pan juices, flour, wine or cream, if preferred, and serve. Some like to cook the bird uncovered to obtain a crisp skin; omit added liquids but be careful it does not burn.

POTTED FOWL

One of the earliest methods for cooking game birds (large and small)—as well as chicken, meats, fish or large game—was "potting it" or "tendering it." This was used on all early frontiers; it kept well.

Cut up the birds small and roll each piece in flour seasoned heavily with salt, pepper and herbs, as desired. Pack the pieces tightly in a large bean pot and cover with boiling water. Place uncovered in slow oven (300°) until water returns to a boil. Then cover and bake for about 4 hours.

WILD DUCK AND OTHER WATER FOWL

The wild duck is probably the most popular of all game birds, though there is much conjecture as to how it should be prepared, cooked and served. The most controversial point concerns cooking time; some say 8 minutes in a "blistering" oven; others, 1/2 hour or longer in a moderate oven. There are arguments about the use of salt or butter and finally, whether or not onions should be thrust into the cavities of all water fowl.

From my experience with duck, I would recommend the following method. To pluck the bird, pour melted paraffin over it and let it harden. Most of the feathers, including the down and pin feathers, will come off when the paraffin is pulled off. The bird should then be singed to remove any remains, and wiped thoroughly with a cloth, which has been dipped in brandy, melted butter or water. Remove the little oil sack from the "pope's nose" and slit open the belly to draw the bird; save liver, gizzard and heart. Clean the cavity with a little salt, rub clean with the cloth and sprinkle salt and pepper on all surfaces. Peel, core and quarter an apple. Peel a few tiny onions and cut a stalk of celery into chunks. Insert these into the cavity. (Some like to add a little currant jelly—or to use currant jelly and omit the onions. Either way is delicious.) Rub the breast and back with a little soft butter, truss securely and put in a roasting pan, breast up. Lay 2 slices of bacon over the breast and, if preferred, a thin slice of orange on top; secure them with toothpicks.

My own experiments have led me to conclude that 20-30 minutes a pound for rare meat and about 45 minutes for better done, is about right. Place bird in a preheated hot oven (450°) and roast for about 20 minutes; then reduce heat to 375°. Baste with a little orange juice, some red wine or, after skimming off some fat, the pan drippings. Baste often and thoroughly. The pan juices will soon evaporate at that heat. Add a 1/2 cup of cold water, skim off as much fat as possible, then add more liquid as preferred: water, orange juice or red wine. Continue cooking to desired doneness, then remove duck to a hot platter and keep warm.

Gravy

Skim off most of the fat from the pan drippings, add flour and blend well. Add chopped giblets and more liquid, if needed. Cook, stirring constantly, until smooth and thickened and serve in a gravy boat.

GAME BIRDS
IN CASSEROLE

1 duck (or hare or grouse or
    any small game bird)
    and giblets
1 thick slice salt pork,
    finely diced
1 tablespoon butter
6-8 wild or green onions,
    chopped
1 clove garlic, mashed
1/2 cup red wine vinegar
2 tablespoons flour
2 cups chicken or veal stock
salt and freshly ground pepper
1-1/2 cups light cream
toast or fine noodles

Sauce
2 sprigs parsley
1 sprig savory
1 tablespoon chopped chives
1 teaspoon dry or fresh mint
1 sprig thyme
1 tablespoon dry mustard
3 tablespoons salad oil
1-1/2 tablespoons red wine
    vinegar

Put diced pork into a heavy Dutch oven and fry slowly until almost melted; heat, add butter and when bubbling brown the duck pieces. Add the onion and garlic and cook until onions are soft. Mix together the vinegar and flour to a smooth paste and add to the pot, stirring in well until the flour begins to brown. Add enough stock to just cover the bird then put lid on pot and cook over medium heat for an hour. Add salt and pepper to taste and prepare the sauce:

Snip all herbs finely (with kitchen shears or pound in a mortar). Add mustard and pour on the oil, stirring vigorously. Add vinegar and beat until well blended. Pour this sauce on the cooked bird. Raise heat again and blend in well then pour on the cream and bring to a bubbling point to heat through. *Do not let it boil.*

Serve immediately over toast or very fine noodles.

ROAST CHICKEN WITH CHESTNUTS

1/2 pound chestnuts (cooked and shelled, see page 51)
6 tablespoons butter
young bird, about 4 pounds, disjointed
1 cup chopped onions
2 teaspoons salt
pinch freshly ground black pepper
1-1/2 cups hot chicken stock or broth

Prepare chestnuts and reserve.
Melt the butter in a Dutch oven or casserole and brown the chicken pieces in it. Add the onions and cook until they are golden. Sprinkle on salt and pepper and half of the broth. Cover tightly and cook over very low heat for 30 minutes. Mix in the chestnuts and remaining broth and simmer gently for 30 minutes longer or until chestnuts are tender. Mash a few chestnuts to thicken the broth and serve over boiled rice, if desired.
Pigeons or other young game birds may be substituted for chicken in this recipe.

CHICKEN POT PIE

This New Amsterdam version of this popular dish is, of course, typically Dutch.

4 slices bacon
1 roasting chicken, disjointed
1 clove garlic, mashed
6 green onions, chopped
2 medium carrots, cut in 1-inch chunks
2 turnips, diced in 1-inch cubes
1 cup chicken broth
1/2 cup apple cider
1 teaspoon each salt and pepper
12 small white onions
2 teaspoons grated nutmeg
1 tablespoon minced parsley
2 tablespoons hard butter
potato dumplings (see page 58) or pastry crust (see page 178)

Heat a large casserole or Dutch oven and fry the bacon until crisp. Remove bacon bits and reserve. Brown the chicken pieces on all sides; then add garlic and green onions and cook until soft. Add carrots, turnips, broth, cider, salt and pepper. Cover tightly and cook very slowly for 30 minutes. (During this cooking, prepare pastry or dumplings and chill.) Add the onions, nutmeg and parsley, cover pot and continue cooking 15 minutes longer. Dot with bits of butter. The liquid should not quite cover chicken; if necessary, add more cider. Drop dumplings by spoonfuls or cover with pastry crust and cover tightly again. Cook for 20 minutes over very low heat; *do not lift cover.* Garnish with chopped parsley and serve in the casserole in which it was cooked.
Variations: Mushrooms and peas may be added, if desired.
Instead of cider, heavy cream may be added before dumplings or crust are put on.

BURGOO

This exotic dish originated as a mainstay of a ship's mess and developed into a potpourri of whatever the cook desired, usually vast amounts suitable for crowds at county fairs and picnics. A tradition at Kentucky Derby Day, it has come to be associated with Kentucky and horse races, hunts and sales, though it has been served at events all over the upper Southland. I have seen recipes requiring 600 pounds beef, a ton of potatoes, 200 ears of corn and so on. Obviously, ours does not.

6 tablespoons bacon drippings
1 pound shoulder of veal, cubed
2 roasting chickens, quartered
4 quarts water
1 tablespoon salt
4 onions, chopped
2 cloves garlic, mashed
8 medium potatoes, diced small
6 stalks celery with leaves, chopped
8 ripe tomatoes, peeled
6 carrots, diced
2 large fresh peppers, chopped
2 cups fresh lima beans
1/4 teaspoon crushed red pepper
4 cloves
1 bay leaf
1 teaspoon fresh thyme
3 tablespoons brown sugar
1/2 teaspoon freshly ground black pepper
2 cups okra pods, sliced
6 cups fresh corn kernels (cut from cob)
1/2 cup butter
1 cup flour
1 cup chopped parsley

Heat half the fat in a large kettle and add the veal; brown well and add chickens, water and salt. Cover and cook over low heat until tender. Remove meat and chickens to a large platter and cool enough to handle. Remove and discard all bones, chop up chicken skin. Return all to kettle. In remaining fat, sauté onions and garlic until soft and add to broth.

Add potatoes, celery, tomatoes, carrots, peppers, beans, seasonings and herbs. Simmer gently for 2 hours, stirring from time to time, then add okra and corn and cook for 15 minutes longer.

Just before serving, rub together the butter and flour until well blended and stir into the Burgoo and cook, stirring steadily, until it has thickened a little. Taste to correct seasoning and sprinkle with chopped parsley.

This recipe should serve about 14-16 people.

Variations: Lean beef may be added as well as cleaned game birds, if desired. The recipe may be doubled or divided successfully.

STUFFED ROASTED CHICKEN À LA GRANDMA TOBIAS

roasting chicken, about 5 pounds
1 recipe potato pancake batter
   (see page 40)
1 cup chopped onions
2 teaspoons salt
1 tablespoon chopped parsley
4 tablespoons butter
1 stalk celery with leaves,
   chopped
1 cup chicken broth

Wipe the chicken inside and out with a damp cloth. Prepare the pancake batter, adding onions, salt and parsley. Rub butter over all surfaces of the chicken and stuff lightly with potato pancake mixture. Close opening with skewers or sew closed. Spread chopped celery over bottom of a roasting pan and put chicken on top. Roast in a moderate oven (350°) for 2-1/2 hours, turning occasionally.

HERBED FRIED CHICKEN

1 frying chicken, about
   3 pounds, disjointed
1/4 cup flour
1/4 teaspoon dried sage
1/4 teaspoon dried thyme
1 teaspoon minced parsley
1/2 teaspoon paprika
1 teaspoon salt
4 tablespoons shortening or oil
3/4 cup chicken broth
1/2 pound fresh mushrooms
   (optional)
2 cups light cream

Wipe the chicken with a damp towel, inside and out. Mix flour, herbs, paprika and salt and dredge the chicken well with the mixture.
Heat a Dutch oven or chicken fryer and add the shortening. When bubbling, arrange pieces of dredged chicken in it and brown the chicken on all sides. Add 1/4 cup of chicken broth and cover pot tightly; reduce heat and simmer about 25 minutes. Turn chicken pieces and continue cooking until tender, about 15-20 minutes longer.
Remove chicken to a warmed platter or serving bowl and keep warm. Discard all but 4 tablespoons of the fat and raise heat. Pour in remaining broth and any remaining seasoned flour (left from coating the chicken); blend well. Slice mushrooms thinly and add. Pour on the cream and, stirring constantly, cook until smooth and thick, then pour over warmed chicken.
Variation: Herbed chicken may simply be fried slowly until quite crisp and eaten with the fingers, without sauce.

ROAST TURKEY

Today our turkeys are so "scrubbed," so tenderized and indeed, almost cooked when we buy them, it is almost impossible to imagine what a dirty job our foremothers must have had when the hunter simply handed them the huge bloody birds, feathers and all, directly from the hunt. A wild turkey of 40 pounds was not unusual, according to reports. The long hunters of the 1700's, cooking out in the open, cleaned the bird thoroughly and made incisions in the skin, into which they stuffed bits of bear's fat, wild herbs and onions. The bird was buried under glowing embers and left to roast overnight.

ROASTING TURKEY

Clean the turkey thoroughly, checking for pinfeathers around the legs and along the wings. Stuff the bird loosely with preferred dressing (see suggestions, page 100), and skewer or sew up and truss bird securely. Rub the surfaces of the bird with butter or rendered chicken fat (or a mixture of fats) and season with salt, pepper and paprika. Put into the roasting pan and cover with oiled paper or muslin or cheesecloth soaked in fat. It is unnecessary to add water to the pan. Preheat oven to 375° and roast at this temperature for 30 minutes. Reduce heat to 325° and turn turkey over. Baste with the pan drippings several times. For the last half hour of roasting, remove the cheesecloth so bird can brown nicely.

Time of cooking:

8-10-pound stuffed bird
    requires 4 to 4-1/2 hours
12-14-pound stuffed bird
    requires 5 to 5-1/2 hours
18-20-pound stuffed bird
    requires 6-1/2 to 7-1/2 hours

More time may be needed so test for doneness. Grasp end of leg bone and move about; it should, if done, move easily in its socket.

Gravy

Remove giblets and neck and, in a heavy saucepan, cover with water or water and dry white wine (about 2 parts water and 1 part wine). Then add a teaspoon salt, a few peppercorns, a few sprigs fresh parsley, 1 carrot, 1 medium onion stuck with 2-3 cloves. Bring to a boil and cook briskly for 2 minutes. Skim off the froth, reduce heat and cover the pan; simmer for an hour. Remove giblets, strain the liquid and cook steadily to reduce it to about 1 cup. Chop the giblets and reserve.

When turkey is ready, add the pan juices to giblet broth. Thicken gravy with a tablespoon of flour and a tablespoon butter (or the yolk of an egg) and cook, stirring steadily, until nicely blended and thickened. Taste to correct seasoning and add the chopped giblets. Pour into a gravy boat and serve with turkey.

TURKEY HERB MIXTURE

This mixture may be used in turkey stuffings and gravies or rubbed inside the cavity of the bird.

The herbs favored for use with turkey are sage, marjoram, savory, thyme and, occasionally, rosemary; a careful mixture of these, plus parsley, can work wonders for all wild fowl. The proportions I find best are:

2 parts sage
1 part each: marjoram, savory and thyme
1/4 part rosemary
4 parts parsley.

If used dry, add 8 parts salt and 2 parts pepper and blend thoroughly. The result is an herbed salt seasoning that costs dearly in the markets. A touch of magic added to this is 1 part dried lemon peel, finely ground and well blended in. If fresh herbs are used, it is best to add them separately.

HERBED TURKEY PIE OR STEW

A particularly fine old use of leftovers.

5 tablespoons turkey fat or butter
1/3 cup flour
1-1/2 cups turkey stock or gravy
1/2 cup milk
1 teaspoon salt
freshly ground black pepper
1 clove garlic, mashed
3/4 teaspoon turkey herb mixture
2 cups diced turkey meat
1/2 cup cooked peas
8 button mushrooms, sliced
1 pastry crust (see page 178)

Melt the turkey fat in a large saucepan and blend in the flour. Stir in the turkey stock and the milk. Cook until lightly thickened, stirring steadily. Add the seasonings, herbs, turkey and vegetables. Blend and pour into a baking dish (about 20x6x2). Roll out the pastry dough, cut into 6 squares 3-1/4-inch) and arrange them over turkey mixture. Bake in a hot oven (425°) for about 35 minutes and serve hot.

SUGGESTED STUFFINGS FOR POULTRY AND WILD GAME BIRDS

All the following stuffings (or forcemeats, as they were called), are adapted from cookbooks of the 18th and 19th centuries.

WILD RICE STUFFING

3 tablespoons butter or bacon fat
1 tablespoon salad oil
1 medium onion, chopped
1-1/2 cups raw wild rice
1 cup broken walnuts
2 cups chopped celery
bird giblets, chopped
1 teaspoon each minced parsley
   and thyme
1/2 teaspoon minced sage
1 teaspoon salt
freshly ground black pepper
4 cups boiling chicken broth

Melt butter with oil in a heavy skillet or large saucepan and sauté the onion until soft. Add rice and cook, stirring often, until slightly colored. Add the walnuts, cook 5 minutes, stir in celery, and cook until rice is golden. Stir in herbs and seasonings.
Pour on the boiling liquid, and simmer until liquid is absorbed, about 30 minutes, and rice is just barely done.
Amounts may be adjusted to the size of the bird. This recipe should stuff a 15-pound turkey.

OYSTER STUFFING

1 loaf white bread
1/2 pound butter
2 small onions, chopped
1 stalk celery, with tops,
   chopped
3 tablespoons minced parsley
1 teaspoon fresh thyme leaves
2 teaspoons salt
freshly ground black pepper
1 pint oysters in liquor

Crumble the bread quite small. Melt butter in a saucepan and add the onions and celery; cook until onions are soft and beginning to show color. Stir in the bread crumbs, add parsley and thyme, salt and pepper. Drain oysters and heat the liquor to boiling point. If oysters are large, cut it half, if small, use whole; add to liquor and cook until the edges start to curl. Drain promptly and stir oysters into bread mixture.
This should stuff a 10-15 pound turkey.

CORN BREAD STUFFING

giblets from bird
water to cover
1 corn bread recipe
  (see page 31)
1 loaf white bread
1 medium onion, minced
1 stalk celery, minced
1 pound pork sausage
1 teaspoon poultry herb
  seasoning (see page 99)
salt and pepper
2 eggs, beaten light
1/2 pound butter, melted
1 tablespoon chopped parsley

Simmer giblets until tender. Drain, reserving broth, and chop giblets. Cut both loaves into 1/2-inch cubes and toast lightly. Add the onion and celery. Separately, brown the sausage and pour off excess fat; add sausage to bread mixture. Stir in herbs and seasonings, broth, giblets, eggs, butter and parsley. Stir to blend well and stuff loosely into cavity of a 10-pound turkey, duck, goose or chicken. Divide recipe in half for smaller birds.

ITALIAN GREEN SAUCE FOR STEAMED OR BOILED FOWL

1 tablespoon minced capers
2 anchovies, mashed
4 green onions, minced
1 clove garlic, mashed
1 tablespoon minced basil
1 tablespoon minced parsley
1 pinch rosemary
1 tablespoon olive oil
2 teaspoons lemon juice
1 twist lemon rind, minced
salt

Blend all together and beat well. This is also delicious on meat and poached fish.

CURRANT SAUCE FOR ROAST FOWL

1 cup hot gravy or pan drippings
1 cup currant jelly
Combine, heat and serve.

MUSTARD SAUCE FOR BOILED OR STEAMED POULTRY OR GAME

3 tablespoons butter
1 tablespoon minced onion
2 tablespoons cider vinegar
2 teaspoons dry mustard
1 tablespoon water
1 egg yolk
1/2 cup pan drippings
1/2 cup cream

Heat butter and sauté onion until soft. Add vinegar and simmer gently for 5 minutes. Moisten the mustard with the water and blend in. Stir in egg yolk, and cook over very low heat stirring constantly for 8-10 minutes. Blend in the cream, heat—but do not boil—and serve very hot.

MEAT, MEAT PASTIES AND CURED MEATS

Pork was the mainstay of frontier meat eating. The animals were easy to feed and often took care of themselves, feeding on acorns and nuts on the hillsides. Moreover, there were more by-products from every part of that animal: skin, feet, tail, ears, head and all the "inwards."

Other domestic animals were slaughtered only as a last resort: sheep were saved for their wool, cows for milk, butter, buttermilk and cheese, domestic fowl for their eggs and feathers. Young girls were given a goose to raise and pluck, to keep the feathers for a dowry; nothing could compare with a goose-down comforter!

• *Marinating* is the process of steeping or soaking meats in an herb-and-spice laden liquid for the purpose of tenderizing and adding flavor. If done at room temperature, the marinade penetrates faster and is perfectly safe for all meats (for a few hours). Poultry, fish and "inwards" or variety meats should be kept chilled. Marinades are made of wine or vinegar, or both, with preferred herbs and spices added.

• *When using wine,* be sure to bring to a rolling boil before reducing heat and further cooking, to evaporate the alcohol. It is the wine flavor that is wanted, not the alcohol. If using cognac, brandy or other hard liquors, flame them (warm, then light) to get rid of the raw alcohol flavor.

• *Browning and searing* meat before adding liquid helps to seal in the juices; it also adds to the appetizing flavor and appearance.

• *Parbroiling* is not so favored now for fear of the caloric content of meat cooked in its own juices. It is simply the dry-heat method of cooking meat by direct contact with the pan's hot metal. Thin cuts cooked by this process are much juicier and more tender. After heating pan very high, add the meat, reduce heat and turn a few times. Many sprinkle on a little salt as soon as soon as the pan has heated, though it is not necessary. Season when done and serve immediately.

• *Servings by the pound:*

1 pound boneless lean meat should give 4 servings

1 pound with some fat and a little bone, should give 3 servings

1 pound of meat with normal fat and bone gives only 1 serving

For example: 1 pound round steak gives 4 servings but short-ribs only 1-2 servings.

GENUINE
VIRGINIA BAKED HAM

As many of the homemade hams were very dry and salty, they required lengthy preparation before cooking. Soaking for a day and a half was important, with a few changes of the water and perhaps even the last change in milk for a few hours. If very dry and salty, the ham was rubbed first with baking soda, then washed thoroughly and simmered in spicy, herb-scented water until tender. The skin was removed and the ham sprinkled with brown sugar—"beating and rubbing it in with the back of a spoon;" then brushed over with beaten egg, covered with browned bread crumbs, stuck with cloves and baked in a very hot oven. It was served with currant jelly or sauce. That was "Genuine Virginia Baked Ham."

ROAST SUCKLING PIG
(or Ewe or Kid or Boar)

The pig should be no more than 4 weeks old, the younger the better; 12-14 pounds at the most. Baste with cream or olive oil during baking for a crisp skin. A fine old recipe for a big celebration.

1 suckling pig
salt and pepper
sprigs of thyme
minced parsley
powdered sage
fine bread crumbs
1/2 pound butter
1/2 teaspoon sugar

Clean the pig thoroughly and rub salt and pepper over the entire surface, inside and out. Skewer on a spit or set on a raised open grill over a roasting pan in a preheated hot oven (about 400°). When half roasted, about 1-1/2 hours, remove from oven and cool only enough to handle it. Prick the skin with a sharp knife and insert sprigs of thyme into the openings. Sprinkle on the parsley, sage and bread crumbs and return to the oven for another 1-1/2 hours, basting very frequently with the melted butter. Serve with a wine or bread sauce.

Variations: The pig may be stuffed with onion, bread soaked in milk, 1/2 pound sausage, broken up, and a cup of milk or wine. The amount depends on the size of the pig.

Another delectable way is to fill the cavity with faggots of rosemary, parsley and thyme, some whole allspice and cloves.

On the great ranches of the Spanish Americans young pigs ran free on the hillsides around the adobe homes, feeding on the acorns of the California wild oak. They said the flesh "was as succulent and fragrant as if fed on corn and house slops."

For local feast days and special celebrations—and there were many—the young men of the ranches chased the pigs down in an exuberant hunt that usually netted them 10-20 pigs to be stuffed with pinenuts and herbs and stretched across the barbecue grills.

CRACKLINGS

Use the skin and fat of any fowl or the back skin of a pig. Cut up into squares (small for fowl, larger for pig) and put into a skillet over very low heat; cook gently, uncovered, until the fat is melted. It may take as long as 2-3 hours. When the skin is tender, raise the heat and cook briskly for about 1/2 hour or until crisp. The pork skin should swell up and blister like a fritter; the fowl skins will turn golden. Remove pork skins from pan with a perforated spoon and place on a warm dish, sprinkle on salt and pepper. Save the fat; pour into a crock and let cool and harden. The skin of fowls is made more delicious and the fat will be clarified, if the heat is turned down very low and a chopped onion added to the pan. When the onion is golden, remove it and the crisp skins to a warm dish, and pour the fat into a glass or stoneware jar; it will be rich yellow if from a chicken and white and sweet if from a goose. These cracklings are delicious eaten with new bread; otherwise they have many uses, crumbled into bread dough (see bread recipes) or cornmeal cakes. The fat may be used as the shortening for breads or in which to brown meats.

PORK PLUGGA

A most unusual treat is this "pudding" that originated in old England. It may well be imagined that puddings were favored by the housewife for it meant no more than boiling (or steaming) in the old iron kettle over the fire.

Suet Pastry
4 cups flour
1 cup finely shredded or
  diced beef suet
1/4 teaspoon salt
about 2/3 cup cold water

Sift the flour, and add suet and salt. Rub them well together and moisten with the water, adding it little by little, working the paste until it is smooth. Roll into a long rectangle about 10 by 12 inches.

Filling
3 cups diced fresh pork
2 large onions, sliced thickly
1 tablespoon shredded fresh sage
2 teaspoons salt
1 teaspoon pepper
dash cayenne

Mix and blend well then spread on half the length of the pastry rectangle. Wet the edges of the crust and roll up lengthwise. Wrap the roll in cheesecloth (like a sausage) and tie the ends. Brush with melted lard or butter. Wrap again in muslin or a towel and put the roll into boiling salted water in a deep kettle wide enough for it to lie flat. Bring water to a boil, then reduce heat and simmer like a pudding for 1-1/2 hours or steam for about 2 hours.

To serve, remove the cloth carefully by putting the roll on the edge of a platter; grasp one end of the cloth and deftly roll out the "plugga" as you pull out the cloth. Serve with the following sauce in a gravy boat.

1 cup pork trimmings
2 tablespoons butter
2 tablespoons flour
1 cup water
salt and pepper
dash powdered allspice

Sauté the pork trimmings very slowly; rub the butter and flour together into a paste and stir into the meat. Add the water and blend. Cook until thickened. Add seasonings and cook until the desired consistency.

RIBS AND SAUERKRAUT

Spareribs of beef, veal, lamb or pork were well browned, then stewed with sauerkraut, apples, potatoes and onions, seasoned with juniper berries or caraway seeds—very spicy.

RIBS AND BEANS

Little whites or navy beans (like those used for Boston Baked Beans) were preferred. They were soaked overnight. The ribs were browned thoroughly, the beans, onions and other preferred vegetables and herbs added and the whole baked for a good long time, very, very slowly.

PORK RIND SAUSAGE LOAF

This was a very popular way of using up pork rinds and tough cuts of beef.

2 pounds pork rind
2 pounds boiling beef
3 tablespoons salt
1 teaspoon powdered allspice
1/4 teaspoon grated nutmeg
1 teaspoon dried savory
8-10 small onions

Wash rinds well and put into a deep kettle with water to cover; bring to a boil. In another kettle, cover beef with water and bring to a boil. Reduce heat and simmer until both meats are tender. Drain meats, reserving cooking broths. Then put meats through a grinder. Combine broths, add meats, seasonings and onions and bring to a boil; simmer until onions are just barely tender. Pour into loaf pans and chill thoroughly. Slice and serve with catsup, chili sauce or mayonnaise. It may also be served hot with boiled potatoes.

Should unexpected guests appear, the addition of a few slices of bread with crusts, soaked in the broth and then mashed in with the other ingredients, will stretch this dish in magical fashion; as many as 8 slices may be added without altering flavor too much.

SAUERBRATEN
(German and Midwest Pot Roast)

5 pounds beef (chuck, rump, bottom round, etc.)

Marinade:
1 cup vinegar
2 bay leaves
1 teaspoon mixed pickling spice
2 cloves garlic
2 cups water or red wine
2 teaspoons salt
ground pepper
3 tablespoons fat
3 large onions, sliced
1 large carrot, sliced
2 tablespoons flour (or fine meal)

This is a good way to use up a tough cut. Put the meat into a wide, shallow bowl or dish, casserole or earthenware crock. Cover with vinegar, spices and water or wine; let stand in a cool place as long as 2 days, turning several times each day.

Drain the meat, saving the liquid. Heat a Dutch oven, melt the fat and brown the meat on all sides. Add the marinade (strained or not as preferred), onions and carrot; cover tightly and cook slowly for 1-1/2 hours or until tender.

Remove meat from pot, strain liquid and return to pot; stir in the flour, browning it well to make a rich gravy. Slice meat and arrange on platter. Pour gravy over or pass in a boat.

Variation: Omit marinating and braise meat in apple cider.

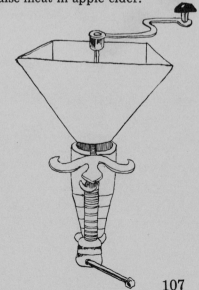

ROASTED WHOLE CALF'S LIVER

1 whole calf's liver
  (about 3-4 pounds)
1 small onion, grated
8 slices bacon
1/2 teaspoon salt
3 leaves sage, finely shredded
1 tablespoon minced parsley
1 sprig thyme, minced
2 tablespoons softened butter

Wipe liver surface with a damp cloth and spread grated onion over the top. Arrange half the bacon slices on the bottom of a baking pan, cover with the liver. Sprinkle on salt and pepper and arrange remaining bacon slices over the top. Bake in a moderately cool oven (325°) for 1-1/2 hours.

Rub the herbs into the softened butter and chill.

To serve liver, slice and cover with a pat of the herb butter.

CARNE CON CHILI
(Now Chili con Carne)

Almost all westerners adore this dish and those who fancy themselves connoisseurs go so far as to stand hard on their own recipe for it, about which they are only too glad to give origin and full details of birth. Texans, in particular, claim it as their native dish and insist it originated there. The Spanish Americans of early California ate the same dish—often without beans—but they inverted the title, making the meat the more important ingredient.

2 pounds boneless beef
1 teaspoon salt
dash black pepper
2 tablespoons fat
Sauce
1/4 pound dry red chilis
4 cups boiling water
2 tablespoons fat
1 tablespoon flour or 2 tablespoons toasted bread crumbs
2 cloves garlic, mashed in salt
1 tablespoon vinegar
olives (optional)

Cut the meat in small dice (do not grind) and season with salt and pepper. Heat a heavy stew kettle and melt the fat; add the meat and simmer slowly until tender, stirring often.

For the sauce, remove the stems of the chilis and cut open; wipe clean inside and place in a heavy skillet or Dutch oven. Pour the boiling water over them and cook until the skins separate from the pulp, then rub through a sieve, to make about 3 cups purée. Heat the fat in the pot, add the flour and the garlic and stir steadily until light brown. Pour in the chili purée and vinegar. Stir, then simmer for 15 minutes longer. Add the cooked meat and cook together for another 12-15 minutes.

This may be garnished with olives, ripe or cured. Serve hot.

PUCHERO (A SPANISH-AMERICAN BOILED DINNER)

On the early California ranches this dish was considered fine enough for the most important guests. Barbecued or roasted beef was very commonplace.

1 knuckle bone, sun and air dried
2 pounds veal
2 pounds beef
4 ears corn
4 sweet potatoes
1 cup garbanzos
2 whole onions
3 dried tomatoes or
   1 tablespoon tomato paste
2 green chili peppers
1 pound green string beans,
   tied in bunches
3 small pumpkins or
   summer squash
1 hard apple
1 hard pear
2 teaspoons salt
1/2 teaspoon pepper

Cover the knuckle bone and meats with cold water. Bring to a boil and skim. Place all vegetables and fruit over the meat, carefully layered in the order given, so they will cook whole. *Do not stir.* Simmer gently until all is tender, about 2-1/2 hours. To serve, lift out the whole vegetables and fruits onto a platter. On a separate platter, place the meat. Strain the broth into a tureen. Serve all very hot.

NEW ENGLAND BOILED DINNER

This is one of the most famous of pioneer dishes and one of the few that has remained unchanged.

5-6 pounds corned beef
   (brisket was favored)
1/2 pound salt pork
herb bouquet: 1 bay leaf, 1 stalk
   celery with leaves, 3 sprigs
   parsley, 2 sprigs each, thyme
   and marjoram (optional)
8 medium carrots, scraped
4 medium turnips, peeled
   and quartered
8 small potatoes, peeled
16 tiny white onions, peeled
   (or 8 medium)
1 small head cabbage, cut into
   8 wedges
8 small beets, scrubbed and
   trimmed

In a very large kettle, cover beef with cold water and bring to a slow boil. Reduce heat, skim thoroughly and simmer for 2 hours. Then add the salt pork and continue slow simmering for 2-3 hours longer or until beef is tender. Add the herb bouquet, carrots and turnips and cook for 15 minutes; add the potatoes and cook for 15 minutes; then add the onions and cabbage and cook until all vegetables are tender. Meanwhile, in a separate saucepan, cover beets with cold salted water and bring to a boil, reduce heat and continue cooking until tender, about 35 minutes. Discard herb bouquet. Serve beef and salt pork on a very large platter and surround with all the vegetables in a pretty pattern. Horseradish sauce is traditionally served with it (see page 148).

SHEPHERD'S OR HUNTER'S PIE

SEA PIE

Dough-enclosed confections, inherited from many European cultures, were a passion on all frontiers and a more complete food unit cannot be imagined. When people knew nothing—and cared less—about calories, pies were a means of economizing, or making the meat go further. The most famous examples of the meat pie are, of course, the English steak-and-kidney-pie (or pudding) and the Shepherd's pies, the latter made with a crust of mashed potatoes rather than pastry.

2 pounds hot cooked potatoes
3 tablespoons melted butter
1 cup hot scalded milk
1 teaspoon salt
pinch black pepper
4 cups cold cooked lamb or beef, diced in 1-inch cubes
1 cup gravy or rich stock
cold butter

Mash potatoes so they are light and fluffy and, gradually, beat in the melted butter and scalded milk, salt and pepper.
Arrange the meat in an oven-proof baking dish (or Dutch oven) and spread the gravy over it. Spoon the potatoes over the meat, then roughen the surface with a fork. Dot the top with bits of butter and bake in a very hot oven (425°) for about 25-35 minutes or until surface is golden.

The Sea Pie was an extraordinarily popular dish, it would seem. Every early cookbook gives some recipe for it, but none explains the mysterious name. My own guess is that men going to sea took such a pie as a last taste of meat before the long period of fish eating.

"*A Sea Pie*—Four pounds of flour, one and a half pound of butter rolled into paste, wet with cold water, line the pot therewith, lay in split pigeons, turkey pies, veal, mutton or birds, with slices of pork, salt, pepper and dust on flour, doing thus till the pot is full or your ingredients expended, add three pints water, cover tight with paste, and stew moderately two and a half hours."

Amelia Simmons'
American Cookery 1796

TAMALE PIE

In the southwestern part of the United States, the Tamale Pie is as American as . . . the apple pie of the East.

1 cup cornmeal
4 cups boiling salted water

Add the cornmeal very gradually —in a slow stream—to the bubbling water, stirring constantly with a large wooden spoon. Cook very slowly for 15 minutes, stirring steadily, then cover and set aside.

1-1/2 pounds ground beef
1 large onion, chopped
2 cloves garlic, chopped
2 pounds ripe tomatoes, peeled
1-1/2 cups tomato sauce
   (see page 150)
kernels from 3 ears fresh corn
1 teaspoon salt
2 teaspoons black pepper
1-1/2 teaspoons chili powder
1 teaspoon dried basil
1/2 teaspoon dried oregano
2 eggs, well beaten
dash cayenne
3 slices bacon, diced

In a large heavy skillet, sauté the ground meat, stirring and separating until well browned. Add the large onion and garlic cloves and cook for 15 minutes, stirring constantly; then add the remaining ingredients (except bacon) and cook for only 5 minutes.

Grease a large casserole or Dutch oven and spread a thin layer of cornmeal on the bottom and up the sides. Pour on a 1/2-inch layer of the meat mixture, then another of cornmeal and continue layering until ingredients are used up, ending with the cornmeal. Dot with the diced bacon and bake in a moderately hot oven (375°) for 30 minutes.

MICHIGAN PASTIES

Actually, pies of any kind of meat, fish or fowl were enormously liked anywhere on the frontier. On the first westward stops—Kentucky, Tennessee and Ohio areas—they were reported by travelers, who found them eveywhere, along with the fried or baked "halfmoon" pasty that is still popular in the Middle West.

2 tablespoons melted butter
3/4 pound chopped lean beef
1 cup sliced mushrooms
1 carrot, thinly sliced
1 large onion, diced
1 tablespoon minced parsley
1/4 cup diced green pepper
1-1/2 teaspoons salt
1/4 teaspoon pepper
1/2 teaspoon marjoram
2 medium potatoes, diced
1/4 cup grated cheddar cheese
2 recipes meat pie pastry
   (see page 179)

Mix together in a mixing bowl all ingredients except pastry. Roll out the pastry rather fine and cut into 24 circles about 5 inches in diameter. On 12 of the circles, put 3 tablespoons of the meat mixture on each and cover with the remaining circles; crimp edges tightly or turn over. Put on a baking sheet and bake in a hot oven (400°) until nicely browned, then remove them to cooling racks.

Serve cold or hot.

Variation: The meat mixture may be lightly sautéed before putting on the paste, and the pasty may be fried in deep hot fat.

MEAT, MEAT PASTIES AND CURED MEATS

MINCEMEAT

There were as many recipes for mincemeat or minced meat as there were frontierswomen, and each defended her recipe to the teeth.

Mincemeat may be made with beef, venison, bear, buffalo or other game—for use in pies and pastries or as pressed meat loaf.

2 cups cooked, chopped beef
8 cups chopped apples
2 cups chopped suet
1 cup chopped citron
2 cups raisins
2 cups currants
2 cups brown sugar
1-1/2 cups molasses
3 cups sweet cider
1 cup strong coffee
1 cup beef stock
1/2 cup grated lemon peel
1/2 cup grated orange peel
2 teaspoons each ground nutmeg, cloves, salt and allspice
4 teaspoons cinnamon

Combine all ingredients and stir until well blended. Cook very slowly until all parts are tender and store in "mason jars" (canning jars with tight lids). It keeps very well in a cool place.

STEAMED MINCEMEAT BROWN BREAD

2 cups sour milk
3/4 cup molasses
1/2 teaspoon baking soda
1 tablespoon hot water
1 teaspoon salt
2 cups whole wheat flour
1 cup cornmeal
1 cup mincemeat

Add the sour milk to the molasses. Mix the soda and hot water and add to the milk mixture. Sift salt, flour and cornmeal and beat into the liquids. Finally, beat in the mincemeat. Pour into small molds (or fruit juice cans, about 12-ounce capacity) about 2/3 full. Cover tightly and steam for 1-1/2 hours. Serve hot with lots of butter. This was a fine Sunday night supper to offer guests.

VENISON MINCEMEAT

2 quarts apple cider
2 cups brown sugar
3 cups seedless raisins
3 cups molasses
2 cups dried currants
3 green apples, peeled, cored and chopped
2-1/2 cups chopped suet
4 pounds ground venison
3-1/2 teaspoons salt
1 tablespoon powdered cinnamon
1 tablespoon powdered ginger
2 teaspoons ground cloves
2 teaspoons grated nutmeg
1 teaspoon ground allspice
2 tablespoons brandy

Put cider, sugar, raisins, molasses, currants, apples and suet into a large, heavy pot; cover tightly and simmer for about 2 hours. Stir in the remaining ingredients except brandy and continue to simmer for 2 more hours, stirring from time to time. Stir in brandy and cool. It keeps very well and makes delicious pie, or filling for cookies.

Smokehouses appeared on farms and behind the great houses of the rich. They were log houses, chinked with clay and thatched with shingles or shakes; spaces left between the top logs aided in circulating air. The interior was about 12 feet square with the fire set directly in the center of the earthen floor, and so constructed that sparks would not fly up to catch on the dry wooden roof.

Racks of green wood were erected quite high above the fire, upon which was hung jerky, hams, beef briskets, fish and game—after all had been pickled in huge barrels for the required amount of time. Smoking was often the responsibility of the men of the family, if they were at home, and each had his own secret recipe. Those without smokehouses learned to make use of barrels, furniture crates or old iceboxes (in the later days). Fish and meat are usually preserved in much the same ways, even to using the same smokehouses, the same woods and so on.

CURED MEATS AND SAUSAGES

Among the most valued recipes that frontier people have left for us are their means of preserving foods for safekeeping and for the flavors these processes impart, even in our age of quick freezing and canning. Pickling, corning and smoking are only some of these; sausage-making, potted meats, "soused" foods and many more are all part of that heritage.

The word "corned" in reference to brining or pickling relates to the 16th century description of fine gunpowder. At that time, "corn" meant all grains, and the finest gunpowder, when spread to dry in single grains, was said to be "corned." When beef was cured by sprinkling with salt, it was called "corned beef," for it was first spread to dry and salt grains or "corns" were rubbed into the flesh. When it was later put into a liquid brine, it was still called by the same general name.

Another relationship is that both corned meats and gunpowder require saltpetre or saltpeter, chemically known as potassium nitrate or nitre. It is an odorless powder and though fresh tasting, it is a little bitter. It gives a pleasant blush of color to meat during pickling, but must be used with great care for it also toughens flesh if more than a pinch is used.

The parts of beef usually corned are the boneless brisket, plate, chuck or round, but any part can be cured in this way. Usually 3 to 4 servings can be expected from a pound, but that depends, too, on the amount of fat.

In cooking, corned meat should be brought to a boil slowly, then very gently simmered until tender. However, home-cured meats are often much saltier than the commercial, and the water should be changed several times during cooking. It is wise to taste the meat a few hours after it has been cooking; if it seems excessively salty, add a few beans, a handful of rice or a few potatoes to the water to absorb some of the salt.

FLAVORED SALT

For the salting-down process, this mixture will produce an immeasurably finer result. For 25 pounds of meat, combine:

5 pounds sea salt
2 teaspoons whole peppercorns
4-1/2 tablespoons brown sugar
1-1/2 teaspoons dried juniper
    berries
1 dry bay leaf, crumbled
6 sprigs thyme, leaves only
8 cloves

Mix well, crush or pound in a mortar and use as salt in brines or for dry salting.

TO CORN OR PICKLE BEEF OR VENISON

It is best to cut the meat into 4-6-pound pieces.

Have barrel ready and spread a layer of salt on the bottom. Rub each piece of meat with a mixture of salt and pepper and pack down in layers, covering each with a layer of salt. The top layer should be of salt. Let stand overnight. In the morning pour on the following brine:

For 25 pounds of meat:
3 pounds salt
1/2 tablespoon saltpeter
1/2 cup brown sugar or molasses
1/2 teaspoon baking soda
2 gallons water

Dissolve the ingredients in 2 gallons water, stir until salt is dissolved. Test with an egg; if it floats, fine, if not, add more salt. Pour over the packed, salted meat and, if necessary, pour on more water to cover the meat. Invert a dish over it and put a heavy weight on it, to be sure that meat will not float. It may be used in 2-3 weeks. For 100 pounds of meat, double all ingredients.

TO PICKLE OR CORN BEEF TONGUES

Trim off the roots and rub each tongue with salt; set aside for 24-30 hours, then drain and dry. For each tongue, mix the following brine:

3 tablespoons brown sugar
3 tablespoons salt
1/4 teaspoon saltpeter
1/4 teaspoon cayenne

Mix and sift the mixture, rub it into all surfaces of the tongue and put it into a crock. Each day, rub the tongue with the mixture, turn and add another tablespoon of salt. It will be ready for smoking or eating in 2 weeks, if turned daily.

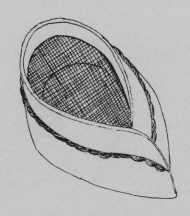

SALTED, DRIED BEEF OR PORK TO KEEP ALL YEAR

For 50 pounds of meat:
4 cups salt
1 tablespoon saltpeter
4 cups brown sugar, packed

Sift and blend all ingredients well. Sprinkle some on the bottom of the barrel or crock and lay down a layer of meat cut into 4-6-pound pieces. Cover with a thick layer of the dry mixture and continue layering, finishing with salt. Cover with a heavy weight and leave for 2 weeks, turning the pieces every day. A liquid will form and if any scum should rise to the top, cover with a thick layer of salt.

The meat may remain in the salt brine and be used from the crock or barrel or, after 3 weeks, the pieces of meat may be taken out, dried and hung, with more salt and pepper added before hanging. This type of cured meat should be freshened like salt fish before cooking, by soaking in fresh water overnight or longer.

CURING PORK
(Hams, Bacon, Etc.)

After slaughtering and cutting up the meat, let it stand and cool a full day, then rub all surfaces with salt. Put down on a bed of salt and sprinkle heavily with more salt. Pack closely in a barrel or large crock or on wooden planks, well weighed down with an inverted dish covered with a clean stone, for from 2-4 days—longer in cold weather and shorter in warm, of course. The salt will have drawn out liquids from the meat, so wipe dry before putting into the following brine:

For 25 pounds of meat:
1 pound brown sugar
2 pounds salt
2 teaspoons saltpeter
1 tablespoon peppercorns
1 cup molasses
1-1/2 tablespoons whole
    pickling spice
2 gallons cold water

Mix all the ingredients except the water and blend well. Then pour on water and stir. Test the strength by dropping in a fresh egg; if it drops to the bottom, add more salt.

With the hand, rub this mixture into each piece of meat and then pack the meat into a large barrel or crock, hams on the bottom, and bacon or side meat on top. Pour on remaining brine and cover with an inverted dish and a heavy weight on top; the meat must not float. Let stand for at least a month for the pickle must penetrate the flesh and bones in order to keep at all. The hams may require even longer than other parts, but a month or

6 weeks is safe enough. Check frequently to be sure no meat is floating and all pieces are well covered by liquid, for the meat must be under brine at all times. When ready, remove from brine, wash under cold running water and dry; then smoke the meat for a few days, 3-4 should be enough in a steady fire with heavy smoke. Remove from smoke and hang for 4-5 days, then cover with cheesecloth bags. It will be ready to eat in about 6-7 months.

Pork chops may also be preserved by the same process, but quite separately, in less time for each stage. Lamb or legs of lamb or mutton may be hung for 3 days after slaughtering then treated the same as pork hams.

MEAT, MEAT PASTIES AND CURED MEATS

TO CURE OR PICKLE SMALL AMOUNTS OF MEAT IN A REFRIGERATOR

4 pounds beef tongue or pork
2 tablespoons salt
3 teaspoons mixed whole
   pickling spice
1 tablespoon brown sugar
3 cloves garlic, minced
1 teaspoon saltpeter

Mix the salt, spices, sugar and garlic together. Rub into the meat thoroughly. Set into a pan, cover well and put into the refrigerator for 3 weeks, turning once a week or more.
To cook, put into cold water and bring to a boil. Discard first water, cover meat again with cold water, bring to a boil and reduce heat; simmer gently until tender.

PASTRAMIZED BEEF

6 pounds beef brisket
1/2 cup salt
1 teaspoon saltpeter
4 tablespoons freshly ground
   black pepper
2 tablespoons brown sugar,
   packed
3 tablespoons mixed whole
   pickling spice
3 teaspoons ground ginger

Mix together the salt, saltpeter, sugar and spices and rub well into the beef. Set into a pan, cover closely and put into refrigerator or very cool place. Turn every few days for 3 weeks, then smoke over a barbecue pit or in a smokehouse—over very low heat —for 4 hours.
It will keep well for some time in a cool place. To prepare, cover with cold water and cook until tender. The length of cooking time depends on how long it was smoked.
A large goose may also be treated in this way; a delicious treat.

POTTED TONGUE

1 pound smoked tongue, cooked
3/4 cup melted butter
1/2 teaspoon grated nutmeg
1/4 teaspoon ground cloves
1/8 teaspoon dried sage
1/4 teaspoon minced parsley
salt and pepper to taste
clarified butter or lard

Dice the tongue and put twice through a grinder. Combine the butter with spices and herbs and blend with the meat. Pack tightly into small crocks or jars and seal each one with a thin layer of clarified butter or melted lard.

SAUSAGE

German settlers had a greater assortment of stored foods than most other emigrants, and used them in a greater variety of ways—and more often. No scrap of meat was discarded; some were smoked, others highly seasoned and still others aged, hanging from rafters over the kitchen fire. The head and feet of the animal were used in making headcheese or souse: the parts were scrubbed and every last bit of fur singed off before the fire. They were then dipped in lye water, boiled for hours and boned. The meat and gristle were cut up into small dice, highly seasoned and, while still warm, pressed to get out as much fat as possible. Headcheese was sometimes pickled, sometimes eaten fresh, but it was always a delicious treat, as everyone reports in letters and diaries.

On their own, southern slaves arrived at a similar method for headcheese; it was a particular favorite for New Year's Day celebrations.

MY FAVORITE SAUSAGE RECIPE

9 pounds lean pork (or
    half pork, half game)
3 pounds fat pork or bacon
3/4 cup fine salt
3 tablespoons rubbed dried sage
2 tablespoons dried
    crumpled savory
2 tablespoons ground pepper
1/2 tablespoon ground cloves
1/2 tablespoon nutmeg
1 teaspoon saltpeter (optional)
2 medium onions, chopped
2 tablespoons white wine
string for tying

Put all ingredients except wine through meat grinder with fine blade, twice. Stir in the wine and let stand for an hour to blend the flavors. Stuff the casings, twisting them every 6-8 inches and knotting as you go. If you plan to use only a few at a time, make two separate knots with a 1/2 inch between, in order to cut off what is needed.

Any meat or combination of meat may be used. The sausages may be smoked, of course, using same procedure as for meat.

To serve, parboil the sausages; simmer gently in salted water for 1/2 hour, then brown in butter. They are also delicious cooked slowly with beans or lentils or served on noodles. Add to soups —vegetable or bean—in slices, about 20 minutes before serving. In a very cool place, they should keep well for several weeks.

Variations: Whole peppercorns, thyme, garlic, chives, coriander, parsley or any combination of these may be added according to taste. Or add pistachio or pine nuts for an unusual touch.

HEADCHEESE OR SOUSE

1 hog's head, cleaned
1 tablespoon salt
1 teaspoon pepper
1/2 cup vinegar
1/2 tablespoon sage
1/2 teaspoon cayenne pepper
1 tablespoon sugar

Cover the head with water; add salt and pepper and bring to a boil; cook until meat is almost coming off the bones. Let cool. Bone carefully and dice rather fine. Put into a round bowl, add remaining ingredients and chill thoroughly. Unmold to serve and cut in thin slices.

VEGETABLES
RICE AND BEANS

The nature of vegetables being what it is, many uses are listed throughout the various chapters. Those mentioned here were indigenous to the continent, and most obviously used on our frontiers: corn, potatoes, both sweet and white, "love apples," squashes of all kinds, beans, Jerusalem artichokes and wild potherbs such as dandelions and wild turnip.

Certain foods were common to all frontiers and foremost was corn. It would be impossible to overestimate the importance of corn in the settlement of America. "Plenty of food" meant plenty of corn, and that was true of the rich, the poor, the northerner and southerner. It grew rapidly even in the poorest soil among rocks and tree stumps, where a plow could not make a furrow for other crops. It grew tall enough to be out of the reach of turkeys and racoons and could not be damaged by snow or rain or small birds, once the ears had developed and were well wrapped in husks.

It may be of interest that in the Jamestown settlement, the legislature passed a law making it mandatory for each planter to set aside a certain number of acres for the growing of corn—to stave off starvation, to feed horses and cattle, as well as for making whiskey!

Among its myriad uses, corn was good at almost every stage of its development: Fresh from the field, showing early milk, it could be boiled, roasted or fried and seasoned only with a little milk, salt, pepper and butter. Even before the milk developed, the pioneers made "gritted corn" by grating the ears to make a coarse meal; the grated kernels were then baked with buttermilk and eggs for a kind of custard. When, in the late fall, the ears grew coarse and hard, kernels were pounded in a "corn pounder," a wooden mortar in which the bottom hollowed-out part was wider than the top opening so that the grains would continually fall back toward the center to be pounded again and again. After sifting, the finest grains were reserved as flour for breads and cakes; the coarser meals, for mush and puddings. One of the earliest recipes for using cornmeal was Hasty Pudding or Cornmeal Mush: "Stir up injun meal and water with a snack of salt and boyle it in a pot."

HOMINY OR SAMP

Obviously of Indian origin, this Southern favorite was made of dried white corn. Hulled corn, the Northern version, was made of yellow corn.

Clean wood ashes were boiled with "plenty of water" until the resulting lye water was strong enough to float an egg. The ashes were discarded and dried corn kernels were tossed into the liquid and boiled until the hulls came off easily. The liquid was drained off and the corn rinsed thoroughly to eliminate all the lye. Finally, it was boiled in clean, salted water until tender. With milk and butter, honey or syrup, it made a delicious supper or was kept in the dairy house until used.

A modern method:
2 tablespoons baking soda
2 quarts cold water
1 quart dried corn kernels

Dissolve soda in the water; toss in corn and soak overnight. In the morning, bring to a rolling boil, reduce heat and simmer, adding water if necessary to keep corn covered, until hulls rub easily off kernels, about 3 hours.

Strain off corn and rinse thoroughly, then rub off hulls between the palms of the hands. Cover with cold water and cook slowly until tender, about 4 hours. Serve as described above.

CORN CUSTARD PIE

1 short pastry crust (see page 178)
2 cups fresh corn kernels
1 cup grated cheddar cheese
8 eggs, beaten
1 cup cream
1 cup chicken broth, boiling hot
1-1/2 tablespoons prepared
  mustard
1 teaspoon salt
1/8 teaspoon pepper
8 slices crisp bacon, crumbled

Combine corn and cheese and sprinkle over pie shell. Combine remaining ingredients, except bacon, blending well. Pour over the corn in the crust. Bake for 30 minutes in a hot oven (425°), then reduce heat to moderate (350°) and bake 20 minutes longer or until nicely browned and a knife inserted near the center comes out clean. Sprinkle bacon over the top. Let cool about 15 minutes before cutting. This may also be made without the cheese.

COLACHE

The Indian name for this dish is *M'sickquatash* but this version is Spanish American.

8 ears fresh corn
2 pounds tender green pumpkin
    or summer squash
2 tablespoons fat or olive oil
2 cups green beans, sliced
2 large tomatoes (or 1/2 cup
    canned), chopped
a clove garlic, chopped
1 medium onion, chopped
2 green chili peppers, chopped
2 cups fresh young lima beans
    (optional)
1 teaspoon salt
1/4 teaspoon black pepper
1 tablespoon vinegar

Strip corn kernels from the cobs. Wash the pumpkin, take out seeds and dice. Heat the fat in a large stew kettle and fry all the vegetables, except corn, very slowly. Add 1/2 cup boiling water if necessary. When the green beans are tender, add the corn and cook for 10 minutes longer.

PUMPKIN AND OTHER SQUASH

A unique symbol of colonial days and Thanksgiving, this native plant lends itself to an infinite variety of uses. Like apples, pumpkins were cleaned and cut in rings to dry; great strings of them were hung from the kitchen rafters and used from fall to fall until the new crop was ready.

SQUASH BLOSSOM OMELET

To make an omelet carefully pick blossoms, wash lightly, sauté in butter and combine with beaten eggs. Cook very lightly.

SQUASH BLOSSOM FRITTERS

The large male blossoms of the squash plants are considered a great delicacy by the Indians, the Spanish and the Italians, among others.

3-6 squash blossoms
1 cup milk
1 tablespoon flour
1 teaspoon salt
1/8 teaspoon fresh pepper
1/2 cup cooking oil

Pick blossoms just as they are about to open.

Combine milk, flour, salt and pepper and beat together until smooth. Put squash blossoms in a large shallow baking dish and pour on the batter. Heat a heavy skillet and add the oil; when hot enough for a drop of water to sizzle when dropped in it, fry the coated blossoms until lightly golden-brown. Drain on paper or on a towel and sprinkle with salt, pepper *or* sugar, according to taste.

SQUASH PIES

The *American Frugal Housewife* by Lydia Maria Child contains the following recipe:
"For common family pumpkin pies, three eggs do very well with a quart of milk. Stew your pumpkin and strain it through a sieve or colander. Take out the seeds, and pare the pumpkin or squash, before you stew it; but do not scrape the inside; the part nearest the seed is the sweetest part of the squash. Stir in the stewed pumpkin, till it is as thick as you can stir it round rapidly and easily. If you want to make your pie richer, make it thinner, and add another egg. One egg to a quart of milk makes very decent pies. Sweeten it to your taste, with molasses or sugar; some pumpkins require more sweetening than others. Two tea-spoonfuls of salt; two great spoonfuls of sifted cinnamon; one great spoonful of ginger. Ginger will answer very well alone for spice, if you use enough of it. The outside of a lemon grated in is nice. The more eggs, the better the pie; some put an egg to a gill of milk. They should bake from 40 to 50 minutes . . . ." (A gill=1 cup)

BAKED PUMPKIN
(Or Other Hard-Shelled Squash)

1 small pumpkin or several
    butternut or acorn squashes
2-3 tablespoons honey
2 tablespoons apple cider
2 tablespoons melted butter

Wash the pumpkin or squashes well and put on a baking tin or dish. Bake in a preheated moderate oven (350°) for about 1-1/2 hours. Remove from oven and cut off the top of the pumpkin, making a hole about 4 inches wide. Scoop out seeds and pulp. Combine honey, cider and butter, spoon the mixture into the pumpkin and replace top; return to the oven and bake for 40 minutes longer. Occasionally, remove top and baste inside with liquid. Serve whole, scooping out portions as wanted. It may also be cut into wedges like a melon. Be sure to spoon a little of the liquid mixture on each serving.

POTATOES

Potatoes, both sweet and white, are said to have been introduced into England by Sir Walter Raleigh at the time of Queen Elizabeth I, which is why the earliest settlers were neither amazed by them nor did they shun them. Potatoes baked in wood ashes were, of course, the favorite way of preparing them. Herb butters are delicious on baked potatoes. Simply mince fine the herbs and add to creamy or whipped butter. Dill, parsley, thyme and sage are excellent choices, but many others may be used.

CRAB LAUDERS

rich pastry dough (see page 178)
6 large sweet potatoes or yams
1/2 pound butter
1 teaspoon sugar
pinch salt

Line 8 small tart or muffin tins with pastry.
Peel the potatoes and boil in very little water until tender.
Drain thoroughly, then return to pot and shake briskly over heat to dry them well. Mash potatoes fine and season with the butter, sugar and a pinch of salt. Fill the tart crusts and cover with top crusts; crimp the edges, prick the tops and bake in a moderately hot oven (375°) until golden brown. These were served as a vegetable.

BAKED SWEET POTATOES AND APPLES
(A New England Feast Day Dish)

2 large apples
2 large, cold cooked
    sweet potatoes
1/2 teaspoon salt
1 teaspoon marjoram
1 teaspoon thyme
2 tablespoons butter
1/4 cup maple syrup

Core, pare and slice apples crosswise. Cut the potatoes into 3/4-inch thick slices. Be sure to have an equal number of apple and potato slices. Sauté the apples in butter until soft and nicely browned on both sides, but still firm. Arrange a layer of potatoes in a large buttered baking dish; sprinkle with salt and finely minced herbs and cover each slice with an apple slice. Pour maple syrup over and dot with butter. Bake in a moderately hot oven (375°) for about 1/2 hour or until all syrup is absorbed and apples are quite brown.

TOMATO

The "love apple," unknown until the discovery of the New World, was considered poisonous by many persons, well into the middle of the last century.

Lydia Maria Child, writing before 1832, states, as if she feared contradiction, that "This is a delicious vegetable." Her recipe for Tomatoes Pie does indeed make a delicious dish. "Tomatoes make excellent pies. Skins taken off with scalding water, stewed twenty minutes or more, salted, prepared the same as rich squash pies, only an egg or two more."

CREOLE TOMATOES

2 tablespoons salad oil
1 tablespoon butter
2 cloves garlic, minced
1 pound fresh okra, stemmed and cleaned
3 tablespoons chicken broth or stock
4 large tomatoes (about 1 pound)
1/2 teaspoon salt
1/2 teaspoon black pepper
1 pinch sugar
1 teaspoon minced fresh rosemary
2 tablespoons minced fresh parsley
1/2 teaspoon powdered allspice

Heat oil and butter together and sauté garlic for 2 minutes. Add whole okra pods and stir-cook for 5 minutes. Add chicken stock and cook for 10 minutes longer. Clean, peel and quarter the tomatoes and add to the cooked okra. Bring just to a boil, reduce heat to a bare simmer. Add seasonings and herbs, cover tightly and simmer for 10 minutes longer. Serve hot or cold. This is sometimes served hot over slices of toasted bread or as a cold relish or side dish with a meat entrée.

BAKED TOMATOES

3 large tomatoes
3 cloves garlic
salt
2 tablespoons butter
6 tablespoons fine cracker crumbs
salt and pepper

Cut each tomato in half, crosswise. Chop garlic coarsely and cover heavily with salt; let stand for 15 minutes, then mash finely adding butter little by little until amalgamated. Melt this in a small saucepan, mix in thoroughly with the cracker crumbs, and spread over the top of each tomato half. Sprinkle with salt and pepper and arrange tomato halves in a shallow baking dish. Bake in a moderately hot oven (375°) for 20 minutes. Serve as a vegetable or a luncheon side dish.

CABBAGE

No matter where the homestead, or what the nationality, cabbage was a most important item in the winter diet of a frontier family. It stored easily and almost indefinitely down-cellar and filled the need for a "fresh" green vegetable all winter. It also proved as good a preventative against the dreaded scurvy as raw potatoes and citrus fruits.

Fresh or pickled, cabbage was an ideal meat accompaniment and a frontier cook with even a little imagination could devise at least twenty ways to use it, from slaws and other salads, to frying, steaming, sautéeing, boiling and baking.

If the sulphurous and malodorous fumes given off during cooking should offend, place a few slices of stale bread on top of the cabbage in a covered pan, if possible. The bread will absorb the odor; discard when the cabbage is cooked. Never overcook cabbage.

A DELICIOUS DISH

"A Delicious Dish. Take a large fresh cabbage and cut out the heart. Fill the cabbage with stuffing, or veal chopped very fine, and highly seasoned, rolled into balls with yelk of egg. Then tie the cabbage firmly together and boil in a kettle for two hours. It makes a very delicious dish, and is often useful for using small pieces of meat."
The American Family Cookbook.
Undated but pre-1840
This "delicious dish" may also be made with a parboiled cabbage, (to soften the leaves); then put stuffing between each leaf, tie securely, and boil in seasoned water.

SWEET AND SOUR CABBAGE

2 tablespoons butter or fat
1 pound soup meat, beef shank or chuck
2 pounds shredded red or white cabbage
1 pound tomatoes, peeled and chopped (optional)
1 small onion, grated
4 quarts cold water
2 tablespoons vinegar or lemon juice
salt, pepper and sugar to taste

Melt the fat in a large soup kettle. Brown the meat and bones and add the cabbage, turning and stirring so all the cabbage is nicely coated with fat. Add the tomatoes and the onion. Pour on the cold water and bring to a boil. Reduce heat and simmer, uncovered, until the meat is tender. Mix the vinegar with the seasonings and pour on, stirring to blend well. Taste to correct seasoning, adding more vinegar or sugar, salt or pepper if necessary. It should be distinctly sweet and sour. The water should have reduced appreciably so it is a vegetable rather than a soup. Remove meat bones, shred meat from bones, return meat to cabbage and stir in well.

MUSHROOMS

These should be picked in the wild only when fully aware of the difference between an edible mushroom, a poisonous mushroom and a toadstool. Too many poisonous ones look exactly like the edible varieties. When buying them in a market, choose those with closed "gills" for they will usually be the freshest. They may easily be dried for future use: string them by the stems and hang in an airy, dark place until completely dry. Store in an airtight jar or crock.

In cooking mushrooms, if planning to serve the caps whole, do not break off or remove the entire stem, but cut off level with the bottom of the cap.

PICKLED MUSHROOMS

3 pounds whole small button
    mushrooms
1 quart water
2 medium onions, thinly sliced
1/2 cup white vinegar
1-1/2 teaspoon salt
1/2 bay leaf
1/4 teaspoon whole peppercorns
1 clove garlic, mashed
1/2 teaspoon ground coriander
1/2 teaspoon dill seed
1/2 teaspoon olive oil

Clean the mushrooms by washing briefly then add to water in a large saucepan. Bring very slowly to a boil, reduce heat and simmer for 6 minutes. Drain off thoroughly and reserve liquid. Slice very thin if large or keep whole if very small. Cut off stems even with bottom of caps. In a tall glass jar, pack the mushrooms in layers alternating with layers of onion. In a saucepan, combine the vinegar, mushroom liquid and seasonings. Bring to a boil, reduce heat and simmer for 10 minutes. Strain and pour over mushrooms and onions. Carefully float the olive oil on the surface. Chill for at least 24 hours before serving.

127

ONIONS

The onion, in all its many varieties, is possibly the most universally used food. It makes superb soup and can be fried, sautéed, steamed, boiled and poached, braised, baked and stuffed.

ONION PIE

1/2 pound butter
3 cups thinly sliced onions
6 eggs, separated
1/2 cup cream
salt and pepper to taste
1 cup white wine
1 rich pastry crust (see page 178)

Sauté the onions very slowly in the butter for 20 minutes, or until transparent. Cool, then stir in the beaten egg yolks, cream, salt, pepper and wine. Lastly fold in the beaten whites of eggs. Mix in each ingredient carefully and thoroughly. Fill a pie plate with the pastry, pour in the onion mixture and bake for 1/2 hour in a moderate oven (350°). Lovely with roast beef.

JERUSALEM ARTICHOKE

There is some question about the strange name of this vegetable—for it is not related to the artichoke nor is its origin Jerusalem. Its Latin specie name is, however, *girasole*, "turning to the sun" or ". . . with the sun," and it is believed that this word was corrupted into *Jerusalem*.

It is, in fact, a member of the great sunflower family, the Helianthus, and a native of the Americas. A tall plant with small sunflower-like blossoms, it is the root that is eaten, raw or cooked, in salads or as a vegetable. The roots are usually left in the ground after the top has been cut back. They are dug up during the winter for use and will re-emerge as plants in the spring without further cultivation.

To plant them, one root is usually sufficient to start with; like the potato, the root has "eyes" from which the new plant grows. One root may have as many as 12-15 eyes and these are cut out and planted.

The American Indians taught the colonists to cook them in soup, much like the potato, though cooked for a much shorter time, and to bake them in hot ashes, each wrapped in a large vine leaf. They may also be sliced thinly and sautéed in butter or bacon fat with minced herbs sprinkled on (parsley, dill, chives, thyme) and salt and pepper.

JERUSALEM ARTICHOKES BAKED IN ASHES

1 pound Jerusalem artichokes
butter or bacon drippings
salt and pepper
large leaves, 1 for each tuber
   (or aluminum foil)

Scrub the Jerusalem artichokes well under running cold water, then rub each one with butter or fat, salt and pepper it and wrap in a large leaf and tie closed. (Aluminum foil may be used in lieu of a leaf.) Place the parcels in the glowing embers of a wood fire (or charcoal) and roast for about 8 minutes, then turn and roast 8 minutes more. Serve with more butter, salt and pepper.

This is a perfect dish for a barbecue; put the parcels in the coals under the meat. It acts as a substitute for potatoes.

SUNFLOWER SEEDS

The sunflower, with its huge blossom atop a tall stalk is sometimes as high as 7-9 feet. The flavorsome sunflower seed, when processed, is a delightful snack. They may be dried in the sun and eaten with a little salt sprinkled on, but as the starch in them is not very digestible, heating seems to improve as well as tenderize the seed covering. For oven roasting simply spread the seeds on a baking sheet and roast in a hot oven (400-450°). A few drops of oil and some salt may be sprinkled on or the seeds may be soaked in a strong salt solution (1/4 cup salt to each gallon of water) before oven roasting. Store in an airtight jar or crock.

WILD GREENS AND FLOWERS

"Salat greens," "sallet" or "salet" are terms found in old cookery books often relating to areas off the beaten track. Generally, it is thought these terms are colloquialisms for salad, but, in fact, they refer to "potherbs" or wild greens.

Those living in wilderness (or near any empty city lot, for that matter) have no need to buy picked-over, days-old salad greens in a market, for the "weeds" of the world produce food for the knowledgeable, wherever they may be. It is, however, very wise to discover which greens to avoid, like poison ivy and oak, very pretty but hardly a culinary treat. Nasturtium leaves and flowers, watercress, wild carrot, corn salad, woodbine leaves, dandelion, radish tops, the curly "pipes" of young fern, wild beet or amaranth, curly dock and sheep sorrel (sourgrass, the children call it) miner's lettuce and purslane are all delicious when very young and very fresh—either quickly cooked or well washed and dried, with a simple dressing and a sprinkling of wild onion or wild garlic over the top.

Actually, most states publish booklets on the wild greens of their state. They cost very little and all one must do is write for them: to the State Capital, Agricultural Division. It is a wise and economical move.

GREENS AND SALT PORK

The traditional way to cook greens (mustard, collard, turnip, dandelion, beet, kale, spinach and chard: wild and domestic) is with ham hock, salt pork or pork jowl. This was especially true in the southern states, but was also used throughout the frontier.

The greens were washed thoroughly and stems cut off.

The salt pork was parboiled in a good amount of water, until tender and the water greatly reduced. The greens were added, with a chopped onion or some garlic, and cooked for 15 minutes; many cooked them for an hour or more, to a purée, but it is hardly necessary and many nutrients are lost.

HERB PUDDING

2-1/2 cups chopped young
   nettles
2-1/2 cups chopped cauliflower
   sprigs
2-1/2 cups chopped cabbage
   leaves
1 cup chopped parsley
3 leeks, both white and
   green parts
1/4 pound pearl barley
2 teaspoons salt, or to taste
1 egg, well beaten

Tie all the chopped vegetables in a muslin bag with the barley and drop into boiling water. Simmer gently for 2 hours. Turn out into a baking dish, add the egg, well beaten, and dot with dabs of butter over the top. Bake in a preheated moderate oven (350°) for about 20 minutes and serve immediately.

Variation: Boil the barley first until transparent, then add the chopped vegetables and tie in the bag. Boil for 30 minutes and finish as above. Any herbs or combination of vegetables may be used.

COUNTRY GARDEN PIE

short pastry crust (see page 178)
2 heads iceberg lettuce
1 bunch each watercress, spinach,
    sorrel, mustard greens and
    beet greens
1 cup chopped chives
freshly ground black pepper
1 tablespoon paprika
2 eggs
1 cup milk
1 cup cream
2 tablespoons flour
1 teaspoon minced parsley
1 teaspoon minced thyme leaves
1/2 teaspoon each minced
    sage and rosemary

Line a deep pie dish with pastry crust. Bring salted water to a boil in a 6-quart pot and toss in lettuce, watercress, spinach, sorrel, greens and chives. Boil for 5 minutes, drain well and chop greens finely, but not into a purée. Stir in the pepper and paprika, and adjust seasoning to taste. Beat together the remaining ingredients and pour them over the greens. Pour this mixture into the pie dish and top with another crust. Prick top crust and bake in a preheated oven (375°) for 35-40 minutes or until crust is golden.

WILTED SALAD

This greatly relished dish was made with almost any green: dandelion tops, lettuce, beet greens and so on.

greens, buds and flowers
bacon, diced
pinch sugar
salt and pepper
vinegar (optional)

Clean greens, buds and flowers and tear into easily eaten pieces. Fry the bacon until crisp. Pour bacon and fat on the greens and sprinkle on sugar, salt and pepper. Toss well to blend thoroughly and serve while still warm. Some prefer a sprinkling of vinegar, as well.

WILD GREENS SAUCE

4 slices bacon, diced large
8 wild onions or 1 small onion,
    minced
1/4 cup vinegar
1/4 teaspoon salt
freshly ground black pepper

Fry the bacon until bits are crisp; remove and reserve them. Sauté the onion until soft and just changing color. Add the vinegar, salt and pepper. Simmer gently for a few minutes. Add bacon bits. Cool for salad dressing or use hot for "wilted greens"; or toss in chopped greens and stir well to blend and cook until greens are done to taste.

FLOWERS AND HERBS
IN SALADS

Salads were often ornamented with flower petals and leaves as much for the lovely appearance as for the nutritious benefits believed hidden in them. Nasturtiums and marigolds were added to salads and salad dressings with a generous hand. The nasturtium leaves have a slightly tart and pungent flavor; a few chopped fine and added to a green salad are delightful.

Those knowledgeable in the ways of herbs and greens, pick dandelions in the fields when they are very young, in the early spring—though they can be used all summer if the tender leaves are carefully selected. When added to salads or omelets they can elevate the most prosaic dish. Or, cooked like other greens, with bacon or salt pork, they are sweet and delicious.

A final suggestion on salads is the addition of herbs, wild or domestic. As a garnish they are very delicate and attractive, but they can also be an intrinsic part of the salad, a vital ingredient: a few sprigs of parsley, rocket or garlic stems, cut fine, can make an ordinary lettuce salad a gastronomic creation!

FRONTIER POTATO SALAD

COLE SLAW

Both potato salad and cole slaw appeared on the "board" at every picnic, church supper, feast day, wedding, "birthing," funeral supper or at the great county fairs and Election Day meetings; in fact, wherever women brought food to contribute to a community meal. Sometimes bits of game were added for extra flavor and each housewife had her own recipe and would make no other.

A most unusual form of Potato Salad is found in the *American Family Cook-book:* "To one pint mashed potatoes (those left over from dinner are just right), add the smoothly rubbed yelks of three hard-boiled eggs, reserving the whites cut in transverse slices to garnish the dish; slice one cucumber pickle, one teaspoon ground mustard, pepper and salt to taste; heat one teacup good vinegar, dissolving in it a lump of butter the size of a walnut; pour the vinegar over the pickle and seasoning, and add the mashed potatoes by degrees, rubbing and incorporating thoroughly. We think you will find it an agreeable addition to the table."

3 eggs
1 tablespoon flour
1 teaspoon salt
pinch cayenne
black pepper
2 tablespoons melted butter
1 quart milk, scalded
1 cup vinegar
1 tablespoon chopped celery
diced, cooked potatoes
garnishes: hard-cooked eggs,
   celery and capers

In a saucepan, beat the eggs very light, add all the dry ingredients and blend well. Then add the scalded milk and, last, the vinegar. Bring to the boiling point and simmer, stirring steadily, until "thick as molasses."
Use half the sauce to pour over potatoes and the chopped celery. Garnish with sliced hard-cooked eggs, celery and capers.
Serve remaining dressing in a sauceboat.

This was often written as "cold slaw" in the old books. An especially fine cole slaw is made with a buttermilk or yoghurt dressing:

3/4 cup buttermilk or yoghurt
1 tablespoon cider vinegar
1 teaspoon sugar
1 small clove garlic, mashed
1 teaspoon salt
1/4 teaspoon coarsely ground
   black pepper
1 stalk celery with greens,
   chopped
1 small onion, thinly sliced
1 head cabbage, chopped or
   shredded

In a bowl, blend together buttermilk, vinegar, sugar, garlic, salt and pepper; set aside for 15 minutes until thickened slightly. Arrange celery and onion slices over cabbage and pour on the dressing. When ready to serve, toss very thoroughly.
For a change of appearance, mix red and white cabbage or use red onion slices. Caraway seeds added give a spicy lift to an everyday dish.

RICE AND BEANS

The wild rice of the Indians who lived in the lake country of the northern plains was always considered a precious commodity; and it may still be found and picked free in many parts of this country. A large, reed-like grass, it grows in three to four feet of water and sometimes rises as tall as eight or ten feet over the surface, with a long flower cluster like a broom on the top. The rice resembles oats and, like it, has a husk which must be removed before it can be eaten. Wild rice can be found in many parts of the country in little ponds and lakes.

It would be hard to improve on the Indian method of gathering it: in a clean canoe or rowboat, paddle out to the plants and pull up armfuls of the reeds so that the heads are over the boat; hit the heads sharply with a stick to dislodge the grains. (If they are too green, they will not separate and if too dry, they will already have dropped into the water, so the time must be gauged carefully.) Spread to dry in a warm, protected place; then put onto cookie sheets in a hot oven (with door open) for about an hour, stirring occasionally so the grains parch evenly. Cool a little, then rub between the hands to loosen

the husks; then store the precious grains in airtight jars. Before using wash thoroughly in many waters to get rid of a smoky dull taste. Wild rice may be cooked like domestic rice, but requires much longer cooking and more liquid.

Both domestic and wild rice may be ground up into meal or flour and used like either corn or wheat meal and flour. For breads, it will not have the gluten or rising powers of wheat but makes superb pancakes, muffins and cookies. It is best used with wheat flour; a combination of one part rice to three parts wheat will still give the unusual flavor of wild rice.

WILD RICE
(Main Dish)

2 cups wild rice, washed well
5 cups water
2 teaspoons salt
8 slices bacon, cut into strips
8 eggs (of wild birds, of course)
1/4 teaspoon pepper
dash hot pepper
6-8 green onions, chopped fine

In a heavy saucepan, place rice, water and half the salt and bring very gently to boiling point. Reduce heat and simmer, uncovered, until all water is absorbed. Fry the bacon in a large heavy skillet, remove the bacon and reserve the drippings.
Beat the eggs with 1 teaspoon salt and the pepper until frothy, then pour into the fat in the skillet; cook pancake-style until lightly browned underneath, then turn and brown on the other side, until eggs are firm; then cut into fine strips and remove from pan and cut into fine strips. Remove rice to a casserole and add eggs and bacon, wild onions and 1/2 cup of the bacon drippings, tossing to blend with the rice. Serve hot.

WESTERN FRIED RICE

1 cup raw white rice
2 tablespoons olive oil
1 onion, minced
1 clove garlic, minced
2 green chili peppers, minced
2 ripe tomatoes, chopped
1 teaspoon salt
dash black pepper

Wash and drain the rice well. Heat the oil in a heavy skillet, add the rice and fry until light golden in color, stirring constantly. Add the onion, garlic, chili and stir until onions are slightly soft; then add the tomatoes, salt and pepper. Stir and fry for 5 minutes longer. Pour on boiling water to cover and put on a tight lid. Place in a hot oven (400°) to steam for 5-10 minutes until dry and fluffy.

BEANS

Baked beans is another in the long list of Indian gifts to the early colonists of New England. As popular today as it was then, the recipe has remained virtually unchanged. In winter, New England women would lay a large piece of muslin in a bowl and pour on the beans. When the beans were cold and hardened to the shape of the bowl, the ends of the cloth were pulled up and knotted and the bundle was hung from a rafter in a shed or cellar and allowed to freeze. For the remainder of the winter, hunks were hacked off for after-church suppers or impromptu meals. In many homes baked beans and brown bread are still eaten hot on Saturday nights and cold on Sunday mornings.

Each state in New England has a particular way with baked beans. In Connecticut a large onion is pushed deep into the heart of the beans and on Cape Cod a half cup of cream is added during the last half hour of baking. In Vermont, maple syrup is used instead of molasses and sugar. Where cooking is done in a fireplace, or a brick oven, the pot of beans is left in the ashes all night.

BOSTON BAKED BEANS

2 cups pea beans or
  "navy beans"
1/2 pound fatty salt pork,
  in one piece
2 teaspoons salt
1-1/2 tablespoons brown sugar
1/4 cup molasses
1/2 teaspoon dry mustard
boiling water

Wash the beans well and discard those that float on the top. Soak overnight covered with cold water. Drain in the morning, cover with fresh cold water and simmer until the skins begin to burst; then pour into the bean pot. Score the skin side of the salt pork and press into the beans, leaving about a 1/4 inch above the beans. Add the salt, sugar, molasses and mustard and pour on boiling water to cover. Cover the pot and bake in a slow oven (250°) for 8 to 9 hours. Add water as necessary to keep beans covered; *but do not stir.* Uncover pot for the last 1/2 hour to allow beans to brown.
This serves 8 for a full dinner with brown bread (see page 37) and butter.

MINERS' BEANS

2 cups pinto beans, washed and
  picked over
5 cups water
1/2 pound salt pork, diced
2 onions, chopped
2 tomatoes, cut up
2 dried chilis, chopped
2 cloves garlic, diced
1 green pepper, sliced

Cook together the beans, water and salt pork for about 2-1/2 hours, or until just barely tender. Add vegetables and seasonings and continue cooking until all water is absorbed and all ingredients are tender. This is generally served with sourdough bread.

FRIJOLES

In the Southwest, the *frijol* usually refers to the "pink bean" or "Mexican brown bean." It is about twice as large as the navy bean and much richer and more nutritious if properly prepared. The secret is to cook it sufficiently, and the oftener it is warmed over, the better it becomes.
The directions are simple enough: simmer 2 cups of dried *frijoles* in water to cover very slowly for at least a full day. They may be eaten thus or fried in hot fat, butter or salt pork or with hot fat, chili sauce and some grated strong cheese mashed in.

CHILI CON CARNE CON FRIJOLES
(A Colonist's Version)

1 pound pinto beans
2 tablespoons olive oil
1 pound lean beef,
  cut in 1/2-inch cubes
1 large onion, minced
2 cloves garlic, minced
2 tablespoons chili powder
1 tablespoon paprika
salt and pepper to taste
boiling water

Soak the beans in cold water overnight. Heat the olive oil in a large Dutch oven and brown the meat in it. Add onion and garlic and cook for 5 minutes. Stir in the chili powder, paprika, salt and pepper, and enough boiling water to cover the meat well. Cook slowly until meat is tender, then remove the meat and cook the beans in the liquid. When beans are soft, return meat to pot and simmer until the sauce is thick.

NAVY BEAN AND BARLEY CHOLLENT

1 pound beef brisket or flank
1 onion, chopped
1 stalk celery, chopped
1 tablespoon salt
dash pepper
2 tablespoons fat
1 large tomato, chopped
   (optional)
1 cup water
2 cups navy beans, soaked
   overnight
1 cup large barley

Trim meat of extra fat; heat the fat in a Dutch oven, then discard pieces. Cut meat in large pieces and brown in melted fat. Add onion and celery and cook with meat until onion is soft. Add remaining ingredients, except beans and barley, and bring to a boil. Skim well, reduce heat and simmer for 15 minutes. Add the beans, cover the pot and cook gently for about 1 hour. Add the barley and more water if necessary and cook for another 1/2 hour. Heat an oven to moderate (350°) and bake for 1-1/2 hours. Be sure the beans are moist at all times. This dish improves with reheating.

LIMA BEANS AND HAM SHANK

In the Midwest and on the prairie, the lima bean was greatly favored, both the large and small varieties.

1 pound dried lima beans
7 cups water
1 ham shank
2 cloves garlic, minced
1 large onion, sliced
1 small dried chili pepper
1 bay leaf
1/4 cup molasses
1/4 cup catsup
1 teaspoon dry mustard
1/2 teaspoon dry ginger
   (optional)
1 pound tiny white onions,
   cooked lightly and drained
1/4 cup brown sugar, packed

Wash beans and either soak overnight or put into a kettle with the water. Bring to a boil and cook for 2 minutes; set aside for 1 hour. Cut the meat off ham shank along the bone and trim off some of the fat, if desired. When beans are ready, add the meat and bone, garlic, onion, chili pepper and bay leaf. Cover and cook for about 1-1/2 hours or until beans are tender.

Remove bone and drain off the liquid, reserving 2 cups of it. Add remaining ingredients, except onions and sugar, to the liquid and mix in with the beans and meat. Pour into a shallow baking dish, add onions and sprinkle on the sugar evenly. Bake in a hot oven (425°) for about an hour.

VEGETABLES, RICE AND BEANS

MILLET

Millet is thought to have originated and been first cultivated in southern Asia over 4,000 years ago. It is of the grass family and is known by many names such as broom-corn, proso, Indian hog millet; other varieties are called barnyard millet, foxtail millet and so on. It is boiled like rice or barley or it may first be browned in a little fat, and liquid added later, as with kasha. Today millet is found in health food stores or Oriental supply stores.

MILLET PILAF

1 cup shelled millet seed
1 medium onion, chopped
1 teaspoon salt
1/4 teaspoon pepper
1/4 cup butter or meat drippings
3 cups boiling water or broth

In a heavy Dutch oven or casserole, over moderate heat, "roast" the millet seed, stirring constantly until golden brown. Then add the remaining ingredients. Be careful; the millet will sizzle. Cover tightly and simmer over very low heat for about 15-20 minutes until liquid is absorbed. Stir occasionally and, if necessary, add more liquid. This should serve about 4 with meats. Barley, kasha or buckwheat groats, rice and very coarse cornmeal or hominy may be used in the same way.

SPANISH GARBANZO BEANS
(or Chickpeas or *Ceci*)

Spanish garbanzo beans are said to have been the first imported food in the New World. When the Spanish settled in Florida, they brought them and planted them; before too long they had been planted across the entire southern part of the country.

2 cups dried garbanzo beans
1 teaspoon salt
lukewarm water
1 cup tomato purée
2 tablespoons olive oil
1 onion, sliced
1 clove garlic, minced
flour
1/2 teaspoon dried oregano
1/2 teaspoon dried marjoram
1/2 teaspoon dried basil
salt and pepper

Wash beans well and put into a deep heavy kettle or saucepan. Add salt and water to cover and soak overnight. In the morning, if water does not cover beans, add more until completely covered and bring to a rapid boil; skim off foam and bring to boil again and skim until completely clear. Add tomato purée, oil, onion and garlic. Cover tightly, reduce heat and simmer gently until beans are tender (about 2 hours). Keep the beans well covered with water, but do not stir during cooking. When tender, drain the liquid off reserving 2 cups; in a saucepan add flour and stir to a smooth paste, adding the herbs and seasonings. Add to the beans, heat through and serve promptly.

BULGUR PILAU

Bulgur or cracked wheat was used throughout the country. The Jesuit Fathers in the California missions cooked it with beans and the Cajun and Creoles in Louisiana used it in *pilau*, adding such enrichments as dried currants, fresh grapes and various wild or domestic meats. Like rice or beans, bulgur lends itself to an infinite variety of flavorings. It is said that the early American use of it was learned from the sea captains who stopped in southern ports.

2 tablespoons butter
2 cups bulgur
1 large onion, chopped
3-1/2 cups chicken broth
1 teaspoon salt
1/2 teaspoon minced
   lemon rind
1/2 cup currants, soaked and
   drained or 1 cup halved
   seedless grapes
2 tablespoons chopped parsley

In a heavy large saucepan or Dutch oven, melt the butter. Add the cracked wheat and the onion and sauté lightly. Remove the pan from heat and cool slightly. Add the broth, salt, lemon rind and currants (if grapes are used, add them later) and place over heat again. Bring to a boil, cover pan tightly, reduce heat and cook for about 30 minutes. If grapes are used, add now with parsley; stir in very lightly, heat through and let stand to cool for 5 minutes before serving. Superb with broiled meats or game.

DAIRY PRODUCTS

The making of butter, clabber, yoghurt and cheeses of all kinds was, quite literally, an organic part of frontier and wilderness living. The products of these chores provided food for lean periods; cheese dishes, as well as the simple bread and butter, often made up entire meals, and very satisfactory ones at that.

PASTEURIZATION OF RAW MILK

Should one be using the milk of one's own cow, sheep or goat, the very first step would be to pasteurize the milk to be certain that harmful bacteria is destroyed.

Two methods are used:

1. *The flash process:* The milk is heated to a temperature of 160-165° and kept there for about 1 minute, then cooled to 40°, bottled and refrigerated.

2. *The holder process:* The milk is heated and kept at a temperature of about 140° for 30 minutes, then cooled to 40°, bottled and refrigerated.

The second method is generally preferred because at the lower temperature the milk retains its natural flavor and the enzymes are not destroyed as happens at a higher temperature. The loss of enzymes makes the milk less easily digested by infants.

CLABBER OR SOUR MILK

Clabber, called *dikkemelk* in the Pennsylvania Dutch country, is made with whole milk.

Put 1 quart in a wide, shallow bowl. As the cream rises, skim and keep for other uses. Set the bowl in a warm place, free from drafts, until it solidifies, then carefully pour it into a muslin bag which has been scalded and dipped into cold water. Hang the bag over a sink or bowl, so the whey can drip off. This generally takes about 12 hours.

Carefully remove the contents of the bag and serve with celery salt, freshly ground black pepper and finely minced herbs to taste. Or serve with cream, sugar and cinnamon.

YOGHURT HARRIS
(Derived from Many Recipes)

Yoghurt may be made of whole or skimmed milk with the addition of a "starter" which is simply a small amount of already-made yoghurt, either the commercial product or home-made. From the finished yoghurt a fine cheese may be made. If planning to make the cheese, plan on a larger amount of yoghurt. The following recipe will make about 1 quart of finished yoghurt.

In a 3-quart enamel or glass pan (do not use exposed metal equipment), slowly heat a quart of whole milk until it bubbles and rises to the top rim; remove from heat and cool to lukewarm. Mix 1 tablespoon of the starter with 1 cup of the lukewarm milk and blend thoroughly; then stir it into the large amount of milk. Pour the yoghurt into a glass or enameled bowl, cover with a large dish then wrap bowl and dish in a large heavy Turkish towel or blanket. Put in a warm place, free of drafts so the temperature remains even, and let stand for from 3-5 hours or until it is thick enough to your taste. Before using, chill well.

Salt, celery salt (ground celery seed and salt), a little garlic, mashed or powdered, or finely minced herbs may be added to taste. Or the yoghurt may be mixed with fruit or served on top of fruit.

Be sure to keep one or two tablespoons of the yoghurt for your next batch!

If a thicker yoghurt is desired, add cream or 1/4-1/2 cup dry milk solids when adding the starter.

YOGHURT CHEESE

Yoghurt cheese is a pleasant by-product of yoghurt—a little like a cream cheese and sweet and pleasant with fruit. If the yoghurt stands for some days before using it to make the cheese, it acquires a slightly sharper flavor. It is an excellent base for salad dressings, for spreads and dips, and may be used just as one uses cream cheese.

Put about a quart of yoghurt into a large bowl; add a quart of cold fresh water and stir until blended. Pour into a cloth dripping bag (a pillow slip is fine) and hang over a sink or pail to drip for about 8 hours or until the contents of the bag are firm and dry. Scrape the curds from the bag into a nonmetallic bowl and beat or whip it until smooth. Add about a 1/2 teaspoon salt or to taste. Chill thoroughly before using.

DAIRY PRODUCTS

BUTTER MAKING

Few things in the world are as gratifying as a slice of homemade bread with freshly made sweet butter smeared over it; to add homemade cheese or jam is as close to heaven as most people ever get! In the old days, a churn was almost a piece of furniture; many were whittled at home in winter by the fireside, but just as many were bought or inherited. Today, churns are small and simple enough to screw onto a preserving jar, to be run by hand or electricity.

Butter is made of the pure cream that rises to the top of milk when it has set in a cool place— overnight in summer and at least 48 hours in winter. It should then be skimmed off and churned promptly. Both churn and cream must be quite cold; place the bowl of cream in cold water before setting to work. Churn steadily and if all goes well, the butter should "turn" in about 15 minutes, even with a hand churn. After it has "turned," remove it to a clean bowl and, with 1 or 2 wooden paddles, "work" the butter by pressing it, getting out as much of the buttermilk as possible. *Do not use the hands as it may injure the butter.* Wash the butter continually as you work using cold running water, or many changes of water, until the water runs clear. Finally, pack the butter in a container, pressing down with the paddles to be sure there is no liquid left nor air bubbles. Chill and enjoy!

Buttermilk is delicious and, they say, a great aid to digestion as well as to the complexion; wash your face with it, leave on to dry, then rinse off. It leaves the skin cool and fresh-looking.

CLARIFIED BUTTER

Butter that is "clarified" is much less likely to burn, will keep well much longer and have a more delicate flavor than ordinary butter.

Melt the butter in a heavy saucepan over very low heat until it is completely clear and a white residue has settled to the bottom. Skim off any froth on the top and carefully strain off the clear butter into a thoroughly clean container.

CHEESE MAKING

Since the earliest records of life in farming areas where domestic animals were bred, the making of cheese has been a vital occupation. It used up surplus milk, gave the farmer a product for trade and immediate profit and was a permanent form of food. The milk used may be whole, skimmed or partly skimmed. It may be cows', goats', ewes' or even buffalo milk, or a mixture of any of these.

Cheeses may be fresh or fermented. Fresh cheese is made by the formation of curd, through the action of added rennet, or by natural coagulation or the addition of certain vegetable juices. Fermented cheeses are made of either scalded or raw curds that form soft cheeses or hard ones with heavy crusts that last almost indefinitely. To make soft cheese, the curds are broken up into fairly large pieces; in making hard cheeses, the curd is crumbled into very tiny bits, again and again, even after the fermentation process has begun. For these kinds of cheeses, molds are required and they may be of wood, earthenware, pottery, tin or even reed baskets. Hard cheese often has the moisture forced out thoroughly in a press before being put into the mold, while soft cheese is broken up very uniformly and left in the mold to drain.

The curdling agent, rennet, from the acid "rennin," is a substance extracted from the stomachs of young animals. It can be made by simply soaking the cleaned stomach of an unweaned calf in water and retaining that water to stir into milk. Or, the stomach may be dried till it resembles parchment (and thus keep · indefinitely), and then a small piece is broken off and soaked in water. Pieces of dried rennet 3 inches by 1/2 inch should be soaked in 1/2 cup of warm water for 24 hours. This water will curdle about a gallon of milk.

Modern cheesemakers also use the commercial Junket rennet tablets: 1/4 tablet to a gallon of milk is the usual proportion. Instead of rennet, some cheesemakers use a plant commonly called yellow bedstraw *(gallium verum)*. The flowers and leaves will curdle milk as effectively as rennet.

SIMPLEST COTTAGE CHEESE I

Let milk stand in a warm place until it sours and curds form. Then put curds into a cloth bag or pillow slip and hang until the liquid (whey) has drained out. The curds should then be scraped off the bag and put into a bowl and salted. Cream may be added for a richer cheese. Caraway seeds give it a fine tangy flavor.

SIMPLEST COTTAGE CHEESE II

Pour a quart of milk into a wide, shallow bowl and let stand in a warm place until it is thick and sour. Then pour into a pan and heat very, very slowly, over lowest possible heat, until the whey comes to the top. Pour off the whey and hang the curds in a cloth bag for about 6 hours or overnight. Put into a bowl again, add a heaping teaspoon of salt and mix well. If allowed to hang for a few days, the sour milk flavor will disappear and the cheese will be drier and harder, though "cheesier." Adding cream or whole milk will make it smoother and richer.

DAIRY PRODUCTS

BUTTERMILK COTTAGE CHEESE

Buttermilk also makes a good cottage cheese. It should be allowed to stand and curdle like sweet milk. If it is too sour and the curds have separated, skimmed milk may be added to bring the curds together again as it sours. Simply proceed as for other cottage cheese.

POTATO CHEESE

A great favorite on the frontier and mentioned in almost all the old books.

5 pounds potatoes, cooked
   and mashed
1 pint soured milk
salt to taste

Mix all ingredients and knead very well; then set aside in a cool place for 3-4 days. Knead again and put into a number of small baskets to drain and dry out. Arrange the cheeses—layered and separated by clean paper or waxed paper, plastic wrap or aluminum foil—in large stoneware crocks to stand in a cool place for at least 2 weeks: "the older, the better."
About this potato cheese, Mrs. Child writes doubtfully that it is "much sought after in various parts of Europe. I do not know whether it is worth seeking after, or not."

NEW ENGLAND POT CHEESE

2 quarts thick sour milk (clabber)
1 teaspoon salt
pepper to taste
2 tablespoons soft butter
2 tablespoons cream

Put the milk into an enamel or glass pan, and set in a very warm place (at the back of the stove) or put into a large pan of hot water; leave until the whey has separated from the curds. Spread cheesecloth over a strainer and pour in the milk; lift the edges of the cloth and tie them together and let the whey drain thoroughly. To hasten the process, squeeze the bag dry. There should be about 1-1/3 cups of curds. Blend in the salt and pepper, butter and cream; herbs such as sage, thyme or chives or a little finely minced onion are a tasty addition.

PENNSYLVANIA POT CHEESE
(Somewhat Like a French *Brie*)

Prepare cottage cheese and put it into a stoneware crock or glass jar. Cover well and put in a warm place—perhaps in a kitchen closet—for from 4-8 days, depending on temperature. Occasionally stir it up. Then, put the crock into a pot of cold water and heat it slowly, stirring the contents of the crock constantly, until it is smooth and melted down. Add butter or cream, if desired, and salt to taste. Pour into molds or small jars to cool.

WAYS TO USE HOMEMADE CHEESE

When homemade cheese was always on hand in extravagant quantities, means to vary the flavor were sought and women vied with each other for recipes on how to use it.

CHEESE SPREAD

4 cups dry cottage cheese
1 teaspoon baking soda
1 tablespoon butter
1 tablespoon salt
1 cup sweet cream
caraway or fennel seeds or finely
    powdered sage leaves and
    minced chives

Combine all ingredients except herbs in the top of a double boiler and cook until melted. Remove from heat and beat with whisk or wooden spoon until thoroughly blended and fluffy. Add a few caraway seeds, fennel seeds or a teaspoon of finely powdered sage leaves and a teaspoon or less of minced chives. Store in a cool place.

ENGLISH MONKEY

1/2 cup stale bread crumbs
1 cup milk
2 teaspoons butter
1/2 cup grated mild cheese
1 egg, well beaten
salt
cayenne
powdered mustard

Soak the bread crumbs in the milk for 15 minutes. Melt the butter in a heavy enamel saucepan and add the cheese. Stir slowly until the cheese melts. Add the egg to the bread crumbs and milk mixture and stir in seasonings. Add to the cheese mixture and heat until completely smooth, stirring constantly. Serve on "sippets" of toast.

CHEESES WITH RENNET

A fresh cheese for either immediate use or to keep, is made of skimmed or whole milk with rennet added. It is put into a cool place (60°-75°) and left to curdle for about a day and a half. It may be eaten as is or whipped up until smooth. Salt and pepper, or sugar, may be sprinkled on, as well as fresh minced herbs or chives. It may be salted and dried very quickly in the sun or the oven, molded to a desired shape and stored on open shelves in the cellar. Frequently brushing the surface with beer or brandy results in fine and unusual flavor. The best rennet cheeses are made with fresh whole milk and are as rich as the milk used. The curds which separate from the whey after the addition of rennet are covered with drops of fat or cream that was in the milk. These must be broken down by cutting up or pressing through a sieve into a mold, packed down into a mass, then taken out of the mold and set aside to dry. The room in which the cheese is made and dried should be kept at an even temperature, between 65°-70° at all times. The cheese is turned every day and kept very clean; only experience and personal taste dictate when the cheese is at its best. Experts say that from 9-20 months is the right length of time! A natural cheese is a grayish white; usually color is added.

DAIRY PRODUCTS

CHEDDAR-TYPE CHEESE

1 piece rennet, 1 x 6 inches
1 cup warm water
2 gallons fresh milk

Soak the piece of rennet in the warm water and let stand for 24 hours; discard rennet and add the water to the milk. (Or add 1/2 rennet tablet directly to milk.) Set in a warm place until the curd forms solidly and is entirely separated from the whey, which will appear clear and greenish. Wash hands thoroughly, then gently push and press all the curds to one side and pour off the whey. Pour the curds into a muslin bag and hang it to dry over sink or bowl. After a few hours, press the curds until not another drop can be extruded and pour and scrape the curds into a scalded wooden bowl; chop very fine and very thoroughly. Wet the muslin bag and pour the curds back into it.

Have ready a heavy box with holes evenly drilled in the bottom and place the bag in it. The lid should fit down into the box and over the bag and a heavy weight should be set on top. Set aside for 3 hours. Remove weight, lid and bag and again take out the curds and chop them evenly into cubes about 1/2 inch square, or smaller. Add salt to taste and pack tightly in a scalded cloth. Scald the box and lid, rinse in cold water and put the wrapped cheese in again as before, with weights on it, and leave overnight. The following morning, unwrap the cheese, rub it all over with salt, rewrap in a fresh scalded cloth, and set aside for 24 hours. Unwrap the cheese again, carefully cut off any rough edges, scrape it clean, rewrap in a fresh cloth and return to the pressing box for another 24 hours. Then take off the cloth and set the cheese on a shelf in a cool, dry place and turn it every 7 days. It may now be eaten but improves with age. Every 30 days thereafter, rub it with a rough cloth; 6-9 months aging results in a finer, more interesting cheese. It is wise to keep a written record of activities beside each cheese.

A much more professional product like commercial American cheese may be obtained by using tablets and cheese coloring made by the Chr. Hansen Laboratory, Inc., 9015 West Maple Street, Milwaukee, Wisconsin 53214. They publish a booklet which gives clearly illustrated directions for step-by-step procedures and all the equipment necessary. There is also (for 10 cents) a helpful illustrated cheese chart they very cordially offer to send to all my readers who request it in writing.

SAUCES

Sauces played an important role in the culinary activities of the frontier. To begin with, they extended the food—combined with leftovers and served over potatoes or cornmeal, for example. They were also greatly favored for "sopping up" with bread at the end of a meal or for putting a finishing touch to a dish. And, finally, a sauce or "sass" was a great showpiece for the cook, whenever company sat at her table.

BASIC WHITE SAUCE

4 tablespoons butter
4 tablespoons flour
2 cups scalded milk, cream
    or white stock
1/2 teaspoon salt
pinch white pepper
dash cayenne (optional)
    or nutmeg

In a heavy saucepan of at least 2 quarts capacity, melt the butter over very low heat and gradually work in the flour to make a *roux*, stirring constantly until it foams; it must not change color. Gradually add the liquid and cook, stirring constantly, until the sauce is smooth and thick. Add salt and pepper and simmer for 5 minutes longer.

Variations: For a richer sauce, beat in 2 egg yolks, one at a time. For a thin sauce, use only 2 tablespoons each butter and flour. For a thicker sauce, 6-8 tablespoons each, butter and flour.

BOILED SALAD DRESSING

Boiled dressing was, and still is, the favored dressing for many salads, particularly on farms in the Midwest. Chicken and potato salads, macaroni salads, even fruit salads and compotes received this treatment. Made well and with a light touch, it can be delicious. What's more, it keeps well for outdoor eating.

1 cup white sauce (see
    preceding recipe)
1 egg yolk
1/2 teaspoon salt
1 teaspoon dry mustard
1-1/2 tablespoons sugar
few grains cayenne
1/4 cup vinegar, heated
1 cup whipped cream (optional)

Cool white sauce and beat the egg yolk into it; beat in the dry ingredients and gradually the warm vinegar. The addition of unsweetened whipped cream is considered a very elegant touch.

GERMAN DRESSING

1/2 cup thick cream
3 tablespoons vinegar
1/4 teaspoon salt
few grains pepper

Beat the cream until stiff and slowly add the remaining ingredients, beating steadily.

HORSERADISH SAUCE

2 egg yolks, hard-cooked
3 tablespoons white cider vinegar
2 tablespoons finely grated
   horseradish
1 tablespoon cream
pinch salt
pinch sugar

Rub the egg yolks to a smooth paste and gradually add the vinegar. Work in the horseradish, cream, salt and sugar. Beat well until light and fluffy.

Variations: To the first 3 ingredients, add 2 tablespoons whipped heavy cream, unsweetened, a pinch of salt and a pinch of dry mustard. Or, whip the horseradish into the whipped cream, add the vinegar, salt and a pinch of white pepper and cayenne.

Most often served with boiled or roasted beef.

MAYONNAISE

This should take no more than 7-10 minutes with table fork and bowl, but a whisk makes the work faster.

1 large egg yolk,
1/2 teaspoon salt
1/2 teaspoon dry mustard
1/8 teaspoon freshly ground
   pepper
1-1/2 cups olive oil or salad oil
   (or mixture)
1-1/2 tablespoons vinegar or
   lemon juice (or mixture)

The egg yolk should be completely free of the white. Place it in a deep bowl and add the dry seasonings. Now stir with an even rhythm (so you don't tire!) and drop the oil in, drop by drop, stirring constantly. After a few minutes, as it thickens, a teaspoon of oil at a time will do (and get it done more rapidly). If it becomes too stiff to absorb more oil, add a little vinegar or lemon juice then return to the oil; use all of it. I find it helps to occasionally beat the oil rather than stir it, then return to stirring. It should be completely blended in 5-6 minutes.

If, for some reason, it does not thicken, start with another egg yolk in another bowl and beat in a little oil, then add the already-started sauce and continue as directed.

Variations: A tablespoon of cream added at the end will cut the oiliness a little yet make it smoother and richer.

Some French friends suggest that a teaspoon of hot water added when finished will make it creamier, whiter and more subtle in flavor: it will also keep longer, they say.

GREEN MAYONNAISE

There are many varieties of this sauce, but the simplest and gentlest is this:

1 cup mayonnaise (see
   preceding recipe)
2 tablespoons finely minced
   parsley
1 tablespoon each minced
   chives and tarragon
1 teaspoon each minced
   dill and chervil

Stir mayonnaise, add the herbs and beat well for a few minutes. Very pretty on seafood salads or served on the side. A half cup of sour cream is a delicious addition.

MUSHROOM BASE FOR SOUPS AND SAUCES

Here is a use for those mushroom stems left from recipes that use only caps.

1 large onion, finely minced
1/2 pound mushroom stems
   (or caps), minced
1 tablespoon minced parsley
3-4 celery leaves, minced
1 tablespoon butter (or fat)
1 tablespoon olive oil
salt and pepper to taste
nutmeg

Prepare the vegetables and herbs separately. Heat butter and oil together in a heavy skillet and, over moderate heat, cook the onion just until it is soft; do not brown. Raise heat a bit and add the mushrooms, stirring until moisture evaporates and mixture begins to thicken a little. Reduce heat to lowest possible point and stir in salt and pepper to taste. Add the parsley and celery leaves and cook, stirring, for 2-3 minutes only. Grate in a little nutmeg, stir and remove from heat. Store in a glass jar covered with waxed paper before screwing on the lid. Refrigeration is not necessary as long as it is kept in a cool dark place.

OLD-FASHIONED SOUTHWESTERN BARBECUE SAUCE

(For a 6-8-pound Roast of Beef, Pork or Lamb)

1/2 cup salad oil
4 large onions, chopped
2 large sweet peppers, chopped
4 cloves garlic, mashed
1/2 teaspoon dried coriander
   leaf or powdered seed
8 fresh juniper berries or
   6 dried
2 bay leaves, crumbled
2 pounds tomatoes, quartered
1 cup vinegar
1-1/2 cups water
2 red chili peppers, crushed
2 teaspoons salt
2 tablespoons chili powder
dash cayenne (optional)
1 square bitter chocolate, grated

In a large, heavy kettle, heat the oil and fry the onions and peppers until lightly colored, then add the garlic, coriander, juniper berries and bay leaves and cook for 5-8 minutes longer. Stir in the tomatoes, vinegar, water, peppers, salt and chili powder. Cover the pot and simmer for 45 minutes to an hour.

Uncover the pot and cook briskly 5 minutes longer. Put this mixture through a meat grinder with coarse blade, add the grated chocolate and simmer, uncovered, stirring constantly, for 20 minutes longer.

When cooking the meat, spoon some of the sauce over at the beginning and cook at moderate heat, or a good distance from the fire. Baste with sauce frequently and serve sauce in a boat with the meat.

HERB SAUCE FOR COLD MEAT AND MEAT SALADS

6 sprigs parsley
4 sprigs thyme
1 teaspoon chopped chives
1/2 teaspoon salt
2 vigorous grinds black pepper
6 tablespoons bread crumbs
1 teaspoon dry mustard
1 tablespoon wine vinegar
3 tablespoon fine oil

Chop the herbs very fine and mix with salt, pepper, bread crumbs and mustard. Mix the wine and oil and pour over dry ingredients; stir or beat to blend well.

This is a variation on vinaigrette or French dressing for salads.

FRESH TOMATO SAUCE

2 tablespoons butter or oil
2 tablespoons flour
1 cup strained cooked tomatoes
1 tablespoon grated onion
    (optional)
salt and pepper
pinch dried oregano or basil
pinch nutmeg

Melt the butter in a heavy saucepan and work in the flour until smooth. Add the tomatoes and onion gradually and cook, stirring constantly, until thick. Season to taste with remaining ingredients. This will make 1 cup of sauce and may be increased many times over, in proportion.

TARTARE SAUCE
(For Fried or Steamed Fish)

2 egg yolks
1 cup oil
3 tablespoons vinegar
1 teaspoon sugar or honey
1 tablespoon chopped capers
    (optional)
1 tablespoon finely chopped
    sour cucumber pickles
1 onion, finely grated
1/2 teaspoon black pepper

Beat together egg yolks, oil and vinegar as called for in recipe for mayonnaise (page 148), or substitute 1 cup mayonnaise for these ingredients. Then add remaining ingredients and beat together very thoroughly until stiff and smooth.

NASTURTIUM SAUCE

This was much admired and served with boiled mutton.

1/2 pound butter
1 tablespoon flour
cold water
1 tablespoon pickled nasturtium
   seeds (see page 159)

Melt the butter over low heat; do not brown. Mix the flour with enough water to form a stiff *roux* and blend with the hot butter. Stirring constantly, add the nasturtium seeds and bring sauce just to the boiling point. Promptly remove from heat and serve.

DRAWN BUTTER

An old-fashioned and delightful sauce to use over vegetables, broiled meats and fish.

3 tablespoons butter
2 tablespoons flour
1 cup boiling water
1/4 teaspoon salt
dash cayenne
1-1/2 tablespoons lemon juice or
   cider vinegar

Melt the butter and stir in the flour; cook a minute or two. Gradually add the boiling water, stirring until smooth. Add the salt, cayenne and lemon juice and serve—in the fanciest bowl you have.

SWEET CREAM DRESSING

1 egg
1/4 cup cream
2 tablespoons sugar
1/4 teaspoon salt
pinch fresh black pepper
2 teaspoons cider vinegar
   (with or without herbs)

Beat egg and cream together lightly. Add seasonings, beat again, then beat in the vinegar. Variations: Add a pinch of sugar. Or use above recipe, but in lieu of 1 egg, use 2 egg yolks and add a pinch of sugar. A pinch of crushed fennel seed is very nice.

TO MAKE SOUR CREAM FROM SWEET

1 pint heavy sweet cream
2 tablespoons cider vinegar
1 tablespoon lemon juice
1 teaspoon salt

Pour the cream into a deep bowl and sprinkle on the vinegar, lemon juice and salt. Stir lightly and set aside in a warm place for 1 hour or until curdled or thickened.
Beat vigorously until stiff and smooth. Serve on fruit salad, fruit puddings and desserts.

SOUR CREAM SALAD DRESSING

1 cup sour cream
2 tablespoons vinegar
vigorous grind black pepper
herbs as desired, depending on
   salad and taste

This dressing is particularly nice on potato salad, on cucumber salad (with dill weed), on mixed vegetable salads and on wild greens salad. Add salt to the salad rather than to the dressing.

PICKLES AND PRESERVES

GENERAL NOTES

It is wise to remember that fruits and vegetables cannot improve in quality after they are picked; choose fresh, firm-ripe produce, free from blemishes, for they can spread and destroy an entire batch. Wash all produce gently but thoroughly; a speck of dirt can start bacterial action. Drain well.

As for spices and condiments, it is best to use fresh and whole ones; old powdered spices sometimes lend a musty and unpleasant flavor. Fine table salt may have unwanted additives. Try to find and use what is labeled as "kosher" salt, which is coarse but unadulterated.

Use a good, clear vinegar, free from sediment and with 4-6 percent acetic acid (most are about 5 percent). Cider vinegar may slightly darken fruit, but white distilled vinegar of standard quality will keep the original color. In boiling too long, vinegar may lose some of its acid which is vital to the keeping qualities of pickles. If a mild-flavored product is preferred, lactic acid will give the necessary acidity for safekeeping though not the sharp vinegary flavor; substitute lactic acid for a part of the vinegar, for example, in proportions of 2 cups vinegar to 1/4 cup of lactic acid.

Either cane or beet sugar may be used; brown sugar will give a richer, darker color and a stronger flavor. This should be dictated by taste.

Either soft or hard water may be used; water containing a good part of iron will cause some darkening, but is perfectly safe to use.

At one time, alum was added to pickles of all kinds to keep them crisp, but we have found that it is not necessary and it will, in time, if too much is used, soften the pickles and cause digestive disturbances in some people. The amount needed in home preparation is so small that it has been found best to eliminate it completely.

Finally, it is wisest to follow recipes for pickling and canning assiduously to avoid spoiling—or at least to follow the proportions given, adding and subtracting with great care, to the last detail. With a little experience and these few recipes, one can soon pickle and preserve any vegetable or fruit one may have in surplus.

Wash jars, lids and screw bands in hot soapy (or detergent) water and rinse very well. Keep the clean jars in boiling water until used, but for not less than 15 minutes.

WINE VINEGARS

The best wine vinegars are made from the best wines, or those which have not had preservatives added. They are very simply made. Gather what remains in glasses or bottles and keep only lightly covered in a warmish place until a light veil appears which is formed by a fungus; this is the "mother" that will grow thicker and larger and should not be disturbed. When the vinegar is strong and acid enough, it may be drawn off into other bottles.

A GOOD VINEGAR

7 pounds brown sugar
3 gallons soft water
2 yeast cakes
2 slices toast

Boil the sugar with 2 gallons of water and skim as the foam rises. Boil for 10 minutes, then remove from the fire, add the remaining water and strain into a barrel or large crock. Spread the yeast on the toast and add to the liquid. Set aside in a warm place and stir each day for 8 days. On the ninth day, cover with cheesecloth (or cover the bunghole with it) and set the crock or barrel in the sun. Let stand for about 6 months.

If the "mother" from old wine is put into it before setting it out in the sun, the time will be shortened. Use when it seems strong enough for you, but do not stir up the "mother" which will drop to the bottom.

A QUICK VINEGAR

This old recipe came to me from a friend working in the hill country in Arkansas.

2 quarts good apple cider
1 cup dark molasses
1/2 yeast cake

Pour the cider into a large kettle or 5-6-quart saucepan. Add the molasses and yeast and stir vigorously to blend them. Stand in a warm place for 24 hours, when it should have begun to ferment. Pour off into an earthenware crock or jug and set aside, uncovered, for 7 days. The dregs will have settled and the clear "vinegar" must be drawn off very carefully—or siphoned off—into small bottles. Cover tightly.

CIDER VINEGAR

This is simply made by letting cider sour naturally in a warmish place. The longer it stands, the more acid it will become. Many ciders have preservatives added and they will never make very good vinegar. Check labels when you buy cider and buy only the finest.

HERB-FLAVORED VINEGARS

These were once made in great variety and for many uses, among them as cold beverages and to "revive flagging spirits." Now herb vinegars are generally used only for salad making, the most common being tarragon, basil, dill and caraway, though mint, burnet (for a cucumber tang), marjoram (to flavor meats), rosemary, parsley or any of the long list may be made according to taste and preference.

Actually, there is now a great revival of toilet vinegars for the complexion, such as rose, violet, lavender and rosemary—once a *must* on the dressing table of "great beauties." As a finishing touch, they leave an alkaline coating on the skin to counteract the effect of allegedly harmful acids and water minerals.

To make any of these vinegars—whether adding leaves, flowers or seeds—simply cut off leafy tips just before the plant comes into bloom and pack them into a wide-mouthed jar; *bruise* the herb with a pestle, potato masher or other instrument and pour vinegar (hot or cold, white, red or cider) over the herb to within 2 inches of the top and cover tightly. Put the jar in a warm place for about 10 days, shaking it up once a day. Then taste the vinegar to be sure it is strong enough for you; if not, strain out the vinegar and repeat the process. When strong enough, filter the vinegar through muslin or filter paper into a nice bottle.

When using a mixture of herbs, be careful to choose ones that will not overpower each other: both chervil and marjoram, for example, are easily subdued by such herbs as basil, tarragon, any mint or chives and garlic. A delicious combination is made up of equal parts of basil, burnet, lovage leaves and 2 parts of parsley. Another is made of 1 part tarragon, 2 parts parsley, lemon thyme and chives. Garlic vinegar is best made without other herbs.

VINAIGRETTE
(True French Salad Dressing)

Use 1 tablespoon of herb vinegar to 3 tablespoons of salad or olive oil with a pinch of pepper and dry mustard and 1/2 teaspoon salt.

Herb vinegars are also useful in marinades for meats, such as sauerbraten and game.

PICKLES AND PRESERVES

PICKLES AND RELISHES AND BUTTERS

An American cookbook without a chapter on pickling fruits and vegetables is inconceivable. The importance of pickling on frontiers is obvious from the frequent mention of it in old writings. At the end of winter or on the trail, when diets consisted largely of salted meat and fish, pickles offered a vibrant note, and it was noted that "children and menfolk could get through a barrel of pickles faster than a hog through clover!"

PICKLED CUCUMBERS

"To Pickle Cucumbers. Let your cucumbers be small, fresh gathered, and free from spots; then make a pickle of salt and water, strong enough to bear an egg; boil the pickle and skim it well, and then pour it upon your cucumbers, and stive them down for twenty-four hours; then strain them out into a cullender, and dry them well with a cloth, and take the best white wine vinegar, with cloves, sliced mace, nutmeg (as much as you please) boil them up together, and then clap the cucumbers in, with a few vine leaves, and a little salt, and as soon as they begin to turn their colour, put them into jars, stive them down close, and when cold, tie on a bladder and leather."

American Cookery
Amelia Simmons 1796

BREAD AND BUTTER PICKLES
(or Sweet Pickle Chips)

4 quarts cucumbers
4 medium onions
1/2 cup salt
1 quart vinegar
2 cups sugar
1 teaspoon ground mustard
2 teaspoons celery seed
2 teaspoons powdered turmeric

Slice cucumber and onions, but not too thin (about 3/8 inch thick), arrange in layers, and sprinkle salt over each layer. Set aside for 3 hours, then drain thoroughly and rinse well. Combine vinegar and seasonings and bring to a boil in a good-sized saucepan or kettle. Add the cucumbers and onions and cook for 5 minutes. Pack into hot sterilized jars and seal tightly.

KOSHER DILL PICKLES

36 small firm pickling cucumbers
8 tablespoons salt
1 quart warm water
10 cloves garlic
3 teaspoons whole pickling spice
1 large stalk fresh dill

Scrub each cucumber with a stiff brush under cold running water. Then pack them tightly in an upright position into glass jars. Dissolve the salt in warm water, then cool. Divide the garlic, pickling spices and dill among the prepared jars. Pour on the cooled salt water and enough fresh cold water to cover the cucumbers and fill the jars to overflowing. Let stand 3-4 minutes to be sure water fills interstices between cucumbers and add more water, if necessary. Seal tightly with scalded lids. Store in a cool, dark place for 6-8 days. If preferred very sour, keep longer. If preference is for half-sour, eat promptly or refrigerate. They will "ripen" progressively of course, but will keep well for months, providing the pickles were unblemished in the first place and the jars clean.

MIXED MUSTARD PICKLES

2 quarts cubed cucumbers
2 small onions, chopped
6 sticks celery, chopped
1 cauliflower, separated into
   flowerets
4 green tomatoes, cubed
2 green peppers, cut in strips
2 quarts water
1/4 cup salt
1/2 cup flour
1/2 cup brown sugar
2-1/2 tablespoons dry mustard
1 tablespoon powdered turmeric
4-1/2 cups vinegar
1 tablespoon celery seed

Put all the vegetables, water and salt in a large bowl and leave overnight. In a large enamel kettle, mix together the flour, sugar, mustard and turmeric and slowly add enough vinegar to make a smooth paste. Then stir in remaining vinegar and bring to a boil; add celery seed and boil for 5 minutes, stirring constantly. Drain the vegetables and add to spices; bring back to boiling and simmer for 5 minutes or until the vegetables are crisp-tender. If vegetables are not covered by liquid, add more vinegar. Pack hot, into hot sterilized jars and seal immediately.

PICKLES AND PRESERVES

PICKLE CHOW-CHOW
(A Pennsylvania Dutch Recipe)

2 quarts green tomatoes, sliced
1 tablespoon white mustard seed
1/2 tablespoon black
   peppercorns
1/2 tablespoon celery seed
1/2 tablespoon whole allspice
1 teaspoon powdered turmeric
1/2 cup brown sugar
1/2 cup water
2 quarts small white onions
   peeled
2 quarts barely ripe string
   beans, sliced
12 cucumbers, chopped
12 green peppers, chopped
1 large head cabbage, chopped

Slice the tomatoes and let stand overnight in salted water. In a skillet combine the seasonings, sugar and water; bring to a boil, add all other ingredients and bring back to boiling point. Cover and simmer, stirring occasionally, for about 10-15 minutes or until vegetables are tender-crisp. Cool slightly and ladle into containers with tight lids.

In the old days, the instructions read to "cook for 3 hours" but I prefer a crunchy relish to a mush.

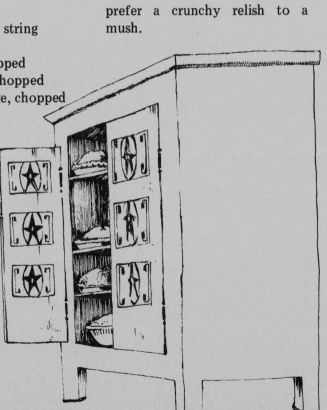

PICKLED
WATERMELON RIND

4 quarts watermelon rind,
   cut into 2-inch squares
2 tablespoons salt
boiling water to cover
4 cups vinegar
8 cups sugar
1/4 cup broken stick cinnamon
1 tablespoon whole cloves

Peel the squares of melon rind and trim off the pink pulp.

Toss rind into a large enameled saucepan with the salt and boiling water. Simmer until the rind is tender when tested with a fork. Drain well and cover with cold fresh water; soak for at least an hour, although it may be left overnight. When rind is chilled and ready, prepare a syrup by combining the vinegar and sugar and bringing to a boil. Tie the cinnamon and cloves into a muslin or cheesecloth bag and add bag to the syrup. Drain the rind and put it into the syrup. Simmer until the rind becomes transparent. Remove the bag of spices and pack the hot rind into hot, sterilized jars. Pour on the boiling syrup to cover well and seal jars at once.

PICKLED PEACHES, PEARS, APRICOTS, NECTARINES OR FIGS

It is well to use small-sized fruit; be sure it is of good quality and in prime condition. Reject blemished fruit or any with soft spots.

4 quarts small fruit
whole cloves
6 sticks cinnamon, broken
8 cups brown sugar (or mixed with white)
4 cups vinegar

Stick about 4 cloves into each piece of fruit. Combine cinnamon sticks, sugar and vinegar and bring to a boil; boil for 2 minutes. Put the fruit into the syrup gently and boil very slowly until soft; *it is best to cook only a few of the fruits at one time.* Lift fruit out carefully and pack into hot, sterilized jars. Cover with syrup and seal immediately.
Figs must be covered especially well with syrup.

SPICED CRAB APPLES

In New England these were traditionally a part of the Thanksgiving dinner.

2 quarts crab apples, with stems
3 cups vinegar
3 cups water
6 cups sugar
1 tablespoon whole allspice
1 tablespoon broken stick cinnamon
1 tablespoon whole cloves
1 teaspoon ground mace

Wash the crab apples, but do not peel or core; leave on stems. Combine the vinegar, water, sugar and spices in a large saucepan and boil until the syrup will cling to a spoon, when dipped in and drawn out. Add the apples to the syrup and reheat slowly to keep skins from bursting. Simmer until apples are tender, then pack them into hot sterilized jars. Pour on the boiling syrup to cover fruit and seal tightly.

PICKLED NASTURTIUM SEEDS I
(False Capers)

True capers were a great extravagance and very difficult to obtain. These did very nicely as a substitute.
Pick the nasturtium seeds when fully formed after the flower has died. Set them in a dry, dark place for 3-4 days after gathering; then put them into a crock or jar and pour on enough boiling cider vinegar to cover them well. Cool and seal tightly. Leave jars in a cool, dark, dry place for about 5-6 months before using. Some directions advise picking them with a short length of stem.

PICKLED NASTURTIUM SEEDS II

Lay the seeds in cold salted water for 2 days after picking (2 tablespoons salt to each quart of water). Then drain seeds and place them in fresh cold water for another day. Drain well and put seeds in a glass jar. Cover with vinegar heated to the boiling point, and seal the jar tightly. These may be eaten in a few days.

PICKLES AND PRESERVES

CORN RELISH

4 cups fresh corn kernels
1/4 head cabbage, shredded
1 sweet red pepper, chopped
6 stalks celery, chopped
1 cup cold water
1 tablespoon salt
1/4 cup sugar
1 tablespoon dry mustard
1/2 cup white vinegar
1/2 cup water

Cook the corn until tender; drain well and reserve. Combine the cabbage, pepper and celery in a large saucepan and add the cold water; cover and cook for 5 minutes. Drain thoroughly and add the corn. In a bowl, mix together the salt, sugar and mustard; stir in vinegar and water and pour over the vegetables. Bring to a boil and cook for 15 minutes, stirring frequently. Ladle into sterilized jars and seal well.

CHILI SAUCE OR RELISH

This recipe was used by the earliest settlers in Point Richmond, California, the Foster family, who still make it up each year.

1 gallon peeled tomatoes, cut fine
4 large onions, cut fine
4 large green peppers, cut fine
1 small bunch celery, cut fine
1 cup sugar
1 cup vinegar
2 teaspoons salt
1 teaspoon ground cinnamon
1/2 teaspoon ground cloves
1/2 teaspoon ground allspice
2 cloves garlic
1 tablespoon mustard seed

Cook tomatoes, onions, peppers and celery in a large enameled kettle until thickened, about 2 hours. Stir frequently. Add sugar, vinegar and spices and cook for about 1/2 hour longer. Pack in sterilized jars and store in a cool, dark place. Sauce will fill about 12 jars.

SAUERKRAUT

Part of the cabbage grown in every frontier garden was put up into sauerkraut. The cabbage was shredded on a cabbage cutter, a board with a sharp knife-blade inserted horizontally or at an angle. The cabbage was salted heavily and packed into a large barrel or earthenware jug, a layer at a time. As each layer was put in, it was pressed down with a wooden board, cut to fit into the barrel, until a salty brine came out of it, which was not removed. When all the cabbage was packed in tightly, the barrel was covered with a clean cloth and a board placed over it and weighted down to keep the cabbage under the brine. The barrel was then set in a warmish place so the contents could ferment. After a few days the brine would start to bubble and emit an unpleasant odor; a scum that rose to the surface was skimmed off carefully. Then it was left to sour and moved to a cold place, at which time it could be eaten or kept almost indefinitely.

SAUERKRAUT
(In Quart Jars)

1-1/2 gallons finely shredded
   cabbage
1 teaspoon sugar (optional)
2 tablespoons salt

Mix and blend all ingredients in a large bowl. With a potato masher mash the cabbage until juice collects on the bottom. Cover bowl with a cloth and set aside for 3 hours. Then firmly press the kraut into 3 sterilized quart jars and push down as hard as possible; pour on the liquid from the bowl. Cover each jar very lightly for the kraut must ferment; let stand at room temperature for several days. Open jars and press down again. If necessary, make a salt solution (1/2 cup salt to 1 quart water) to fill the jars to the top with liquid. Now screw on lids tightly and store jars in a cool, dark place. It is usually ready for use in about 4 weeks.

GRAPE VINE LEAVES

large but young grape leaves
2 quarts water
4 teaspoons salt
1 cup lemon juice (optional)

Be sure leaves are unblemished. Wash each leaf well, then pat dry and lay flat, one on top of another; make piles of 25-30 leaves and cut off stems. Roll up each stack of leaves and tie with string.

Bring water, salt and lemon juice to a rolling boil and drop in bundles of leaves, a few at a time. Cook for 1-2 minutes, no more, and remove promptly. Pack bundles in tall jars, tightly, and pour on boiling liquid to cover well. Seal tightly.

If they are to be kept for a long time, they should be processed like canned fruit. If kept in a cold place, they will keep well for several months.

To use: lay each leaf out flat. Use any forcemeat as for example: ground meat and rice, pilau, kasha, etc., to taste; put a spoonful on each leaf, roll up like an envelope and lay, seam down, in a casserole or Dutch oven. Roast, bake or braise. Serve hot or cold. Nasturtium leaves may also be treated this way.

PICKLES AND PRESERVES

TOMATO CATSUP

Catsups are made of fruit or vegetables and used as relishes, like chutneys, with meat.
This recipe is adapted from *The American Family Cook Book* which is undated but obviously pre-1850.

2 gallons tomatoes
2 tablespoons salt
1 tablespoon powdered mace
1 tablespoon black pepper
1/2 teaspoon cayenne pepper
1 tablespoon ground cloves
4 tablespoons ground mustard
2 cups vinegar

Cut each tomato in half and put into a large enameled saucepan or kettle; cook until the pulp is all dissolved then strain well through a fine sieve and pour back into the kettle. Bring to a boil and add all seasonings *except vinegar*. Bring back to a boil, reduce heat as low as possible and simmer for 5-6 hours, stirring frequently. Take off the heat and let stand for 8-10 hours in a cool place. Stir in the vinegar to blend well, then bottle it and keep in a cool, dark place.

CRANBERRY CATSUP

16 cups sound cranberries
2 cups vinegar
2 cups water
5 cups brown sugar
1 teaspoon salt
2 teaspoons powdered cinnamon
1 teaspoon powdered cloves
1 teaspoon powdered allspice

Combine the cranberries, vinegar and water in a large kettle and cook until skins pop open; put through a fine sieve. Return to the kettle and add the remaining ingredients. Stirring constantly, bring to a boil, reduce heat and simmer for 8 minutes. Ladle into hot, sterilized jars or bottles. Seal tightly.

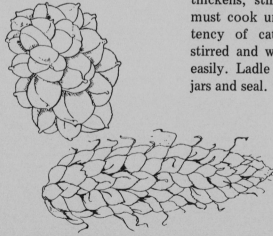

RHUBARB CATSUP

5 pounds rhubarb, cut into
   1-inch pieces
5 pounds sugar
3 cups vinegar
2 teaspoons salt
1 tablespoon black pepper
1 tablespoon powdered cloves
1 tablespoon powdered allspice
1 tablespoon powdered ginger
   (optional)
1 tablespoon powdered cinnamon

Wash the rhubarb, drain lightly and toss into a large kettle. The water which clings after washing is sufficient for cooking. Cook gently until fruit is tender. Drain rhubarb and return to kettle. Add remaining ingredients, stir well and cook gently until it thickens, stirring frequently. It must cook until it is the consistency of catsup, but must be stirred and watched for it burns easily. Ladle into hot sterilized jars and seal.

PICKLED WALNUTS

Pickled walnuts or butternuts are a heritage from English forebears and are still a cherished relish to roast meats. Gather the nuts when they are still tender enough to be easily pierced with a pin.

100 walnuts
2 tablespoons whole cloves
2 tablespoons powdered allspice
2 tablespoons grated nutmeg
1 tablespoon whole peppercorns
1 tablespoon grated ginger
1 tablespoon grated horseradish
1 cup mustard seed
4 cloves garlic, chopped
2 tablespoons salt
vinegar

Wipe the nuts well or scrub with a coarse brush. Mix all spices well. Lay walnuts by layers into a crock sprinkling the spice between each layer. Bring to a brisk boil enough vinegar to cover the nuts well, then pour it over the nut mixture. Cover the crock tightly and set in a cool, dry, dark place for an entire year before using.

PEANUT BUTTER

The subject of peanuts is simply not mentioned in old cookbooks—at least none that I could find. They apparently were of little consequence even in the South before the end of the last century and were used mainly by very poor whites and slaves.

I do remember, however, that my husband spoke often of the wonderful peanut butter his mother made for him when he was a little boy. He assures me she simply shelled roasted peanuts, put them through a meat grinder once or twice and added salt. The labels of today's processed peanut butters list ingredients as ". . . peanuts, hardened vegetable oil, seasoned with dextrose, salt and sugar." It seems to me it needs no added oils or sugars, which leaves us with peanuts and salt, unless the added sweetening appeals to the maker. The peanuts should be roasted before being ground. Spread them on cookie sheets and roast at 300° for about 20 minutes, turning from time to time. Cool quickly. Shell, remove inner skins and grind in a coffee grinder or use the finest blade of a meat grinder. Salt to taste.

APPLE BUTTER

Apple butter has always been associated with the Pennsylvania Dutch. It is a great favorite of all children.

6 quarts cider
10 pounds apples
8 cups brown sugar
2 tablespoons powdered allspice
3 tablespoons powdered cinnamon
2 tablespoons powdered cloves
salt to taste

In an uncovered enameled kettle, cook the cider over high heat for about 30 minutes or until reduced by half. Wash the apples, quarter and core them (do not peel) and add to the cider. Cook over low heat until very tender, stirring frequently. Press the mixture through a strainer and return to the kettle. Add the sugar, spices and salt and cook very, very gently, stirring almost constantly, until it thickens. Pour into sterilized pint jars and seal tightly.

CURING OLIVES

The olive, which is native to warm regions of Europe, Asia and Africa, was brought to the New World about 1770 and planted by Junipero Serra and José de Galves on the grounds of the Mission San Diego. Soon cuttings were planted in most mission gardens. For almost 100 years after it was introduced, the olive was grown only for the oil it produced which was used for lamps, medicine and cookery, especially as a substitute for butter. Only to a very limited degree and for their own use did the padres process the European type of eating olive.

By about 1870, experimental growers were taking cuttings from the old trees and by 1885 the commercial production of olive oil was in full swing. Though the oil they produced was considered as fine as any in Europe, growers had soon to face the fact that they could not compete with the cheap European labor and they turned their attention to the production of pickled ripe olives. A number of pioneers have recorded their impressions of their first taste of the olives that salesmen were trying to popularize.

MEDITERRANEAN BLACK OLIVES

When sufficiently sweet, remove most of the salt and put olives into a clean vessel. They can be left with some salt on them or they can be oiled with 1/2 cup olive oil to each 2 pounds of olives. Stir well so each olive is covered with oil. After 2-3 days, they will be ready to eat. Keep uncovered in a cool, dry place.

Hang the bag or set the basket over a pail so the liquid that forms may drip off. Each day add more salt to replace that which has drained out with the liquid.

After 6 days, take out an olive and taste it. If still too bitter, leave olives in salt for another few days until they have lost their bitterness.

When sufficiently sweet, remove the olives from most of the salt and put into a clean vessel. They can be left with some salt on them or they can be oiled with 1/2 cup olive oil to each 2 pounds of olives. Stir well so each olive is covered with oil. After 2-3 days, they will be ready to eat. Keep uncovered in a cool, dry place.

These olives may, after a few days, be put into jars and covered with a good dry red wine with a 1/2 teaspoon of dill or fennel seeds added, and left for a month or so in a dark, cool place. They are an astonishing taste treat.

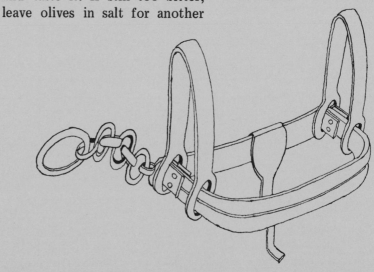

BLACK OLIVES IN BRINE

Olives not washed in lye always keep a certain bitterness much favored by many connoisseurs. Choose ripe black olives of good quality, of medium size and not overripe. Pierce each olive once or twice with a pin. (For convenience, cut a long bottle cork in half lengthwise and push a few long pins, like hatpins, through the cork. The cork can then be held in the hand and the pins pushed down among the olives, picking up a number at a time and piercing them at the same time; do this gently for the olives must not be bruised.) Drop the olives into a large stoneware crock and pour on enough fresh cold water to cover them. Set aside for 10-12 days, changing the water every day. The olives should then have lost most of their bitterness.

Drain the olives and immerse them in the same brine used for Green Spanish Olives. Proceed in same way.

TO PROCESS THE GREEN SPANISH OLIVE

Select pulpy, meaty olives, entirely developed and ripe but still green. Reject any that are blemished or beginning to darken. Measure the amount of olives picked and put an equal amount of good, clean wood ashes into a large stoneware crock, large enough to hold the olives comfortably. Dilute the ashes with enough cold water to form a thin, runny paste and carefully put the olives into it. Gently stir it with a long wooden stick, being careful not to bruise the fruit.

The first day, stir up the mixture 4-5 times bringing the olives at the bottom to the top. Each day thereafter, stir them 2-3 times daily. Each olive should be washed thoroughly by the lye solution. To assure this, take an olive out after a few days and tear the meat from the pit with your fingernail. When the meat comes off very easily and cleanly, it is ready. The time necessary to accomplish this depends on the quality and strength of the solution.

When ready, lift the olives out of the lye with a slotted wooden spoon and wash them in fresh cold water until they are free of the odor of the lye.

Clean the stoneware crock and replace the washed olives in it. Cover with fresh cold water and change the water every day for 8-10 days until the water looks absolutely clear and the olives are free of bitterness. Taste to ascertain the latter.

Now they are ready to be immersed in the following brine:

10 quarts water
2 pounds coarse or rock salt
8 bay leaves
few branches fennel
small piece of orange peel
few coriander seeds

Mix all together well and boil briskly for 5 minutes. Remove from heat and cool completely. Then pour over the clean olives and set aside for 5-6 days. Now the olives are ready to be eaten.

GENERAL DIRECTIONS FOR MAKING PRESERVES AND JELLIES

The directions given by Miss Catherine Beecher in her *Domestic Receipt Book* of 1846 are sufficiently relevant today to be repeated:

"Gather fruit when it is dry. Long boiling hardens the fruit. Pour boiling water over (all) sieves used, and wring out jelly-bags in hot water the moment (before) you are to use them. Do not squeeze while straining through jelly-bags. Let the pots and pans containing sweetmeats just made remain uncovered three days. Lay brandy papers over the top, cover them tight, and seal them, or, what is best of all, soak a split bladder and tie it tight over them. In drying, it will shrink as to be perfectly air-tight. Keep them in a dry, but not warm place. . . ."

All old cookbooks refer to "brandy paper" on top of jars. The paper was actually what would seem to us as a very fine rag-content letter paper. A round was cut out to measure about an inch over the opening. It was then soaked in brandy, fitted to the top of the filled jar and tied down well. The bladder of an animal was thoroughly cleaned, spread flat and soaked until very soft; then it was tied on over the paper. It made an excellent air-tight cover, as good as our own screwtop jar lids.

Certain fruits contain enough natural pectin to make a firm jelly without adding artificial pectin.

Apples, quinces, plums, some grapes and cranberries have more natural pectin than other fruits, especially if slightly underripe; crab apples have the most and were added to other fruits to assure jellying. Today, pectin—powdered or liquid—is commercially prepared from these fruits and is more economical because less sugar is required.

As a general rule, all fruits, except currants, should be picked slightly underripe for jellying and fully ripe for jams. The rule of hand is 20 minutes boiling of juices before heated sugar is added, and 5 minutes after. Sweet juices naturally require less sugar.

Acid fruits require a pound of sugar to a pint of juice after initial cooking and dripping.

Beet or cane sugar may be used equally well, and corn syrup or honey may replace part, though not all, the required amount of sugar. Honey generally produces a darker product than when only sugar is added. When using pectin, always follow directions to the letter.

PROCESSING FOR ALL PRESERVES

Fill hot sterilized jars with the freshly made preserve, adjust the lids and submerge the jars in a wide, deep pan of boiling water, over the fire. When the water returns to boiling, let boil for at least 5 minutes. Remove jars from water, tighten the lids and let cool. Store in a cool, dark, dry place.

APPLE JELLY

apples
cold water to nearly cover
For each cup of juice:
3/4 cup sugar

Clean apples and wipe well. Remove stems and blossom ends; cut in quarters, put into a large kettle and pour on enough cold water to *nearly* cover. Cook over low heat until apples are soft. Turn into a jelly bag of muslin, flannel or cheesecloth and allow the juice to drain off, but do not squeeze. Measure the juice and boil briskly for 5 minutes. Add sugar, stir and continue boiling until the jelly "coats a spoon" (220°). Skim well if froth appears, then pour into jelly glasses. Cover lightly until the jelly has set, then cover the jelly with a layer of paraffin. For 2 pounds apples, the yield is about 4 glasses jelly.

QUINCE JELLY

Wash quinces well, quarter them and remove seeds. Then follow recipe for Apple Jelly. This is a most aromatic and delicate jelly.

MINT JELLY

Follow preceding recipe for Apple Jelly. Just before ready, bruise the leaves of fresh mint and add to jelly. A small amount of green coloring is usually added, but not necessary. When jelly is sufficiently flavored with mint, remove the leaves.

MIXTURES OF APPLES AND OTHER FRUITS FOR JELLIES

Equal amounts of apples and rhubarb, apples and strawberries, apples and cranberries or apples and cherries all make delicious jellies; 1 part quince or barberry to 3 parts apple is also very effective. Follow recipe for Apple Jelly—adding all fruits together from the beginning.

CURRANT JELLY

Wash the currants but do not remove stems. Put into a large kettle and add water to cover by about 1/4 inch. Cook until the currants are soft and transparent or colorless, then strain through a jelly bag. Use 3/4 cup sugar for each cup of juice and proceed as for Apple Jelly.

DRIED APPLE JELLY

When and if jellies ran out in mid-winter, this recipe was a godsend.

1 pound dried apples
water
5-1/2 cups sugar (approximately)
3/4 cup lemon juice

Wash the dried apples and soak overnight in cold water to cover well. In the same water, cook the apples until soft and strain through a jelly bag. Measure carefully and add an equal amount of sugar and the lemon juice. Boil until the jelly coats a spoon. Pour into jelly glasses and pour on melted paraffin.

WILD GRAPE JELLY

Wild grape vines are found almost all over the country, flourishing where least expected. In New England, the wild grape, currant and wild beach plum were the favorite fruits for jellies. Select fruits that are just barely underripe. Wash and drain well and put them into a large kettle. Mash well and cook until the juices flow freely; then strain through a jelly bag. Add 3/4 cup sugar for each cup juice and boil until it "sheets" from the edge of the spoon—about 15 minutes or so. Pour into hot sterilized jars.

WILD ROSE HIP JELLY

An ancient Scottish recipe much used in the earliest inland frontier.

2 cups cut-up rose hips
2 pounds crab apples, quartered
1 pound sugar for each pint
   of juice

Wash rose hips and crab apples; do not peel or core. In a heavy enameled pan, cook them with water to cover, until very soft. Pour into a jelly bag and let drip; *do not squeeze.* Lightly grease a saucepan with sweet butter, pour in the strained juice and 1 pound of sugar to each pint of juice. Boil until the syrup jells when tested in a cold saucer. Pour into hot jars, let cool and seal tightly.

HERB JELLIES

These had been popular in Europe since the Middle Ages. Making them was an art that women took great pride in for they were a thing of beauty and great delicacy. On the frontier, wild herbs were often used and the jellies served with game as well as domestic meats.

2 cups boiling water
4 teaspoons dried thyme leaves
2/3 cup lemon juice or
   fruit vinegars
3 cups sugar
2 large apples, chopped,
   with skin, seeds, etc.

Pour the boiling water over the thyme leaves; cover and let stand 1/2 hour. Strain leaves through double cheesecloth and return to heat. Add lemon juice and sugar. Stir until dissolved. Bring to a boil, add the chopped apple (or other pectin), bring back to a rolling boil and skim carefully and thoroughly. Pour into a jelly bag and let drip into a large saucepan. Before putting into jars or jelly glasses, place a small, young rose-geranium leaf or a peach leaf in the bottom of the jar; pour jelly over slowly and set aside to cool. Pour on paraffin and seal. Pectin may be used instead of the apple; follow package directions.

ROSE PETAL JAM

2 cups rose petals
2 cups warm water
2-3/4 cups sugar
2 tablespoons honey, strained
1 teaspoon lemon juice
rose coloring (optional)

Using kitchen shears, cut off the tough white bases of the petals and cut petals into strips. Pack tightly, being careful not to bruise, into a saucepan. Add the water and cook for 10 minutes, or until soft. Strain off the juice into a saucepan, reserving petals, and add sugar and honey; cook until it "spins a fine thread" (220°). Add the drained petals and simmer gently for about 45 minutes. Stir in the lemon juice and continue cooking gently until it is thickened. Add food coloring, if desired, and pour into small jars. Seal at once.

SUN-MADE STRAWBERRY JAM

Select large, slightly unripe but brightly colored strawberries (about 4-5 quarts may be made at one time). Hull the berries and slice those that are very large. Measure berries and add an equal amount of sugar. Pour fruit and sugar into a large kettle; stir very carefully with a large wooden spoon to avoid mashing until berries are well covered with sugar. Bring to a rolling boil and boil *exactly 3 minutes.* Pour immediately into very shallow trays of glass, china or enamel; the fruit should lie in a single layer with the juice no more than 1/2 inch thick. Cover with panes of glass or mosquito netting and place in full sunshine for 2-3 days; take inside during nights. If moisture collects under the glass panes, turn them over (this may be often at first). The jam is ready if the syrup forms jellied waves when the container is tilted to one side. Bottle immediately.

WESTERN FRUIT JAM

Apricots, grapes, peaches, figs, pears or quinces may be used in this jam. Remove pits of peaches or apricots; peel and core pears or quinces. Use other fruit as it is picked.

Put fruit into a large kettle and cook very slowly until some of the liquid is evaporated, stirring constantly to be sure fruit does not stick or burn. Measure fruit and add equal amounts of sugar; continue cooking slowly, stirring frequently, for about 1 hour or until very thick. Pour out on large platters, trays or baking sheets and spread evenly. Set in the sun until a dryish crust forms. Stir thoroughly and pour into hot, sterile jars, crocks or glasses, and seal tightly. This is probably the simplest way to make a fruit spread and was the usual method used on the frontier.

DESSERTS

CITRUS MARMALADE

8 grapefruits or 12 oranges
water
1 very large tart apple, chopped
1 lemon, sliced thin
1 cup sugar for each cup
   cooked fruit

Slice the fruit thinly; then remove as much white pith as possible but save the skins and sliver them fine. Save a few seeds and tie them in a muslin bag with a long thread. Put fruit into a heavy enameled saucepan, half cover with cold water and let stand overnight. Drain thoroughly the next morning and wash under running water. Again half cover with fresh water, and bring to a rolling boil; reduce heat and simmer for 1 hour.

Taste liquid and if bitter, change water and reboil as before. Add apple, lemon and bag of grapefruit seed and bring back to boil and simmer for 1 hour. Cool slightly, measure fruit and juice and add 1 cup sugar for each cup of fruit and liquid. Stir well and cook for 3/4 hour longer or until it jells when tested on a cold saucer. Discard bag of pits. Pour into jars and seal immediately.

If a clear marmalade is preferred, omit the apples.

PUMPKIN PRESERVES

1 medium-size pumpkin
2 cups sugar
1/2 cup lemon juice
6 cups sugar
2 cups water
1 tablespoon grated ginger root
   (optional)
1 teaspoon grated lemon rind

Cut the pumpkin in half, remove seeds and peel off the rind. Cut into 3/8-inch strips. Put layers down in a stoneware crock with plenty of sugar between layers. Pour on the lemon juice. Let stand in cool place for 2 days. Drain well and discard liquid. Make a syrup of the 6 cups sugar, water, ginger and lemon rind; cook until slightly thickened. Then add pumpkin strips, cooking until soft. Drain off and reserve the syrup and continue cooking until thick, then pour over pumpkin and pack in jars, covering well with syrup. Seal tightly.

TOMATO PRESERVES

5 large ripe tomatoes, peeled
   and finely chopped
3-1/2 cups brown sugar
juice and grated rind of
   1-1/2 lemons
1 tablespoon grated ginger root
   (optional)

Cover tomatoes with the sugar and set aside for 1 hour. Add lemon juice, rind and ginger. Cook over very low heat, stirring almost constantly until it thickens. Test by letting a little cool in a saucer or cup; if thick, it is ready. Pack in jars and seal.

SALPICON

5 pounds dried currants
3 oranges
7-1/2 cups sugar
1 pound raisins

Wash the currants and chop the oranges fine, using the peel of one of them. Cook the currants and sugar for 20 minutes, add the oranges and cook for 5 minutes. Add the raisins and cook 5 minutes longer. Pour into hot jars and seal.

QUINCE HONEY

A lovely old-fashioned recipe, served with hot biscuits or muffins or warmed and spooned over fruit compotes and puddings.

Peel the quinces, reserving peels, and soak fruit in cold water for 10 minutes. Cover the peels with boiling water and boil briskly for 1/2 hour; then drain liquor into large kettle. Grate the quinces, add to peel-liquor and cook for 20 minutes. Skim well, measure the mixture and add an equal amount of sugar. Simmer gently for 10 minutes, then pour into hot jars and seal promptly.

HONEY OF ROSES

1/2 pound fragrant roses
2 cups water
2 pounds strained honey

Cut off white tips of petals and discard. Mash red petals with a wooden potato masher. Add water and boil for 15 minutes. Add the honey and boil to a thick syrup. Pour into hot, scalded jars and seal tightly.

DESSERTS

Desserts on the frontier were generally very limited. When company came, a pudding was put to boiling or baked, and served with a sauce of dried fruit. Doughnuts and fritters were also popular and, if the housewife was particularly dainty, light pies, trifles, fools, flummeries, many with curious names like Tipsy Parson, Berry Grunt, Berry Slump and Apple Pandowdy. The Dutch in New Amsterdam could continue making their great spicy cakes and cookies—or *koekjes*—for they had easy access to spices and exotic liqueurs from distant shores. Inland housewives depended on the house-to-house meanderings of a peddlar and, if money was available, bought a nutmeg or a few blades of mace and some allspice for the delicate puddings of her pride.

It is hardly likely that any cookbook, for a long, long time, was slanted toward the frontierswoman, for few could afford such a luxury even if she needed the high-falutin' advice. I believe the cookbook that gives the clearest clue to frontier recipes is *The American Frugal Housewife, dedicated to those who are not Ashamed of Economy*, in which Lydia Maria Child directs her city-bred readers to buy whenever possible from "friends in the country," in order to get the purest products for the least cash outlay. Actually, frontier recipes may easily be determined by the list of ingredients, for what was made, raised or found on the homestead was most commonly used.

BAKED INDIAN PUDDING

Indian Pudding, either boiled or baked, is still a superb dessert when well made. Remember that "Injun" meant cornmeal.

4 cups hot milk
1/2 cup cornmeal
1/4 teaspoon baking soda
1/2 teaspoon salt
1/2 cup sugar
1/2 cup molasses
1 teaspoon ground ginger (optional)
1 teaspoon ground cinnamon (optional)
1/2 cup molasses
2 cups cold milk

Heat the milk in the top of a double boiler or a large heavy saucepan over low heat. Stirring constantly, pour the cornmeal, in a stream, into the hot milk. Cook for about 15 minutes or until quite thick. Remove from heat. Combine the baking soda, salt, sugar and spices, if used, and stir into cornmeal mixture. Add molasses and cold milk, blending well. Remove to a casserole or baking pan (2-quart capacity) and bake in a preheated moderately slow oven (275°) for about 2 hours. Serve warm with maple syrup, honey or whipped cream and grated nutmeg. This should serve a good-sized party of about 15.

BOILED INDIAN MEAL PUDDING

6 cups milk
2/3 cup sifted Indian meal (yellow cornmeal)
3/4 cup very finely diced beef suet
2 teaspoons salt
4 eggs, separated
1/2 cup white or brown sugar

Scald the milk in a heavy large saucepan, and slowly stir in the cornmeal, then the suet and the salt. Beat egg yolks with the sugar added and add to cornmeal mixture. Beat egg whites until they hold a peak but are not yet quite dry, and add to mixture.
Dip a pudding bag in very hot water and sprinkle it lightly with flour inside and out. Fill about half full with the pudding batter. Tie the bag at the very top, leaving enough room for the pudding to expand. In a large kettle bring water to the boiling point and drop in the pudding bag; continue boiling for 10 minutes, reduce heat and simmer for 5 hours. Serve with a sweet sauce, sugar or maple syrup. This should serve about 15 very generously.

BATTER PUDDING

Batter Pudding was a recipe that appeared quite often; this one is from Miss Beecher's *Domestic Receipt Book.*

4 cups milk
3/4 cup flour
9 eggs
1 teaspoon salt

"Beat the yolks thoroughly, stir in the flour and add the milk slowly. Beat the whites of eggs to a froth and add the last thing. Tie in a floured bag (first dampened with hot water) and put it in boiling water, and boil two hours. Allow room to swell."

STEAMED FIG PUDDING

2 cups flour
1/4 teaspoon salt
1-1/2 teaspoons baking powder
1 teaspoon ginger
1 cup minced beef suet
1 cup finely diced figs
1 egg, beaten
2/3 cup molasses
2/3 cup milk or water

Sift together flour, salt, baking powder and ginger. Add suet and figs. Moisten with beaten egg, molasses and milk or water. Pour into a well-greased mold and cover securely. Steam for 3 hours. Serve with Hard Sauce (see page 177).

TRIFLE
(New England or American Style)

This old English recipe is still being served at church suppers, ladies' club meetings and wherever women contribute to meals for large numbers of people.

Lay a slice of sponge cake on an individual dish, spread with raspberry jam and cover with another slice of cake. Pour on a soft custard (often flavored with almond or almond extract) and cover with whipped cream or *Syllabub* (following recipe).

Trifle may also be made with macaroons instead of sponge cake, soaked in sherry or custard.

SYLLABUB
(Or "Whip Syllabub")

1 pint heavy cream, beaten stiff
1/2 cup sifted fine sugar
whites of 2 eggs, beaten stiff
rind of 1 lemon, grated
1 cup sweet white wine,
    madeira or sherry

After beating the cream, fold in half the sugar; put remainder of sugar with the egg whites. Fold them together and add lemon rind and blend in lightly. Slowly add the wine and serve as a sauce over Trifle (preceding recipe), an arrangement of lady fingers, sponge cake or macaroons. This may also be served over fruit.

TIPSY PARSON

Tipsy Parson was another form of Trifle. Arrange thick slices of sponge cake on individual dishes and sprinkle with a little sherry or madeira. Pour chilled custard sauce over each serving. A little grated nutmeg over it is nice.

DESSERTS

GOOSEBERRY FOOL

1 quart ripe gooseberries
2 cups water
1 tablespoon butter
1 cup sugar
dash salt
2 cups whipped cream
   or unwhipped sweet cream
powdered sugar (optional)

Stem the berries and cook in the water until just tender, then press through a colander to remove skins, if desired. Many served the berries without straining. Add the butter, sugar and salt and stir gently. Fold in the cream and sprinkle on some powdered sugar.

BLUEBERRY SLUMP OR BLUEBERRY GRUNT

4 cups blueberries, well washed
1 cup sugar
2 cups water
2 cups flour, sifted
3 teaspoons baking powder
1/2 teaspoon salt
1 cup milk

Combine berries, sugar and water and cook over low heat until tender. Mix dry ingredients and sift; stir in the milk (to make a "drop dumpling") and drop by spoonfuls into the bubbling berry juice. Cook uncovered for 10 minutes, then cover and cook 10 minutes more. Serve with cream, plain or whipped.

Apple Slump is made by stewing 8 sweet apples with 1/2 cup molasses, 1/2 cup sugar and 1 cup water; proceed as above.

RHUBARB ROLY POLY

2 cups flour, sifted
1 teaspoon baking powder
1 teaspoon salt
2 tablespoons sugar
2 tablespoons butter or lard
3/4 cup milk
2 cups rhubarb, sliced small
1 cup sugar
butter

Sift flour, baking powder, salt and sugar into a bowl and cut in the shortening. Add the milk, bit by bit, to make a soft dough and knead on a lightly floured board; roll out about 1/8 inch thick. Spread with the rhubarb, dot with butter, sprinkle with sugar and roll up the dough carefully, like a jelly roll. Bake in a preheated moderate oven (350°) for about 35 minutes. Serve with cream or Hard Sauce.

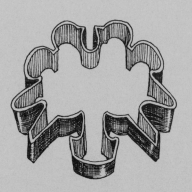

APPLE PANDOWDY COUNTRY STYLE

5 apples, sliced but unpeeled
3 tablespoons sugar
3 tablespoons molasses
1/2 teaspoon powdered
  cinnamon
1/4 teaspoon grated nutmeg
1/2 teaspoon powdered cloves
pinch salt
butter
rich biscuit dough (see
  recipe, page 23)

Spread a layer of apples on the bottom of a baking dish, cover with a little molasses and sugar and a sprinkling of half the spices. Cover with another layer of apples and remaining molasses, and spices. Dot with bits of butter and bake in a moderate oven (350°) until apples are soft. Cover with a crust of biscuit dough and bake for 15 minutes longer in a hot oven (400°) or until nicely browned. Serve with Hard Sauce or Lemon Sauce.

MAPLE SUGAR SAUCE

2-2/3 cup maple sugar, broken
  fine
2-1/2 tablespoons sweet butter,
  in small bits
1 teaspoon lemon juice
  (optional)
pinch salt

Put maple sugar into a heavy saucepan and cook over very low heat, stirring constantly, until a clear syrup forms. Remove from heat and stir in the butter until well blended. Stir in the lemon juice, if desired, and the salt. Serve hot over fruit puddings and compotes.

WINE SAUCE FOR PUDDING

1 cup sherry or madeira wine
1/4 cup water
4 tablespoons sugar
juice of 1 lemon
rind of 1 lemon, chopped fine

Heat the wine and water together; bring to a boil and add sugar, lemon juice and rind. Stir and cook until sugar is completely dissolved. Serve hot over pudding.

HARD SAUCE FOR PUDDING
(Prairie Style)

1/2 pound butter, softened
3 cups powdered sugar
juice of 1 lemon
grated nutmeg

Cream the butter and sugar and beat until light and frothy. Beat in the lemon juice and the nutmeg. Chill.
Adding 2 tablespoons rum or brandy makes it gala indeed.

HOT LEMON SAUCE

1/2 cup sugar
1 tablespoon cornstarch
pinch salt
1 cup cold water
1 teaspoon grated lemon rind
3 tablespoons lemon juice
3 tablespoons butter

Mix sugar, cornstarch and salt; gradually stir in the cold water. Bring slowly to a boil, stirring constantly and then cook gently until thick and clear, stirring steadily. Remove from heat and stir in the lemon rind, juice and butter.

RICH PASTRY CRUST

For fruit pies or other pastries, as desired. Makes 2 crusts.

2 cups flour
1 teaspoon salt
2/3 cup shortening, chilled
5-6 tablespoons ice water
    (use as little as possible)

Sift flour and salt together and cut in the shortening with two knives or a pastry blender until it looks like coarse meal. Sprinkle the water over it and mix lightly with a fork, then work with your hands to form a ball. Chill for 30-35 minutes. Divide the ball of dough in half and roll on a lightly floured board, using quick, light strokes, from the center to the outer rim until about 1/8 inch thick. Line the pie plate carefully, pressing the pastry down with the fingertips.

All pastry dough must be worked as quickly and lightly as possible. The less water used the better; the less your hands touch it, the better. Some believe that all lard, or lard and butter mixed, gives a more flavorful and whiter crust than all butter or other shortening.

If the lower crust is to be baked before it is filled—called a "blind" crust—throw on a handful of rice or a few cleaned pebbles. This is done to prevent blistering. Discard rice and pebbles after baking. Otherwise, the crust should be slashed, but this is not advisable if the filling is runny. Bake 12-15 minutes in a preheated 450° oven.

To test unregulated ovens for pies, place a sheet of paper in the oven when it is preheated. If it turns a delicate brown, then the oven is right.

OLD FASHIONED CRUST

For pies or to enclose a fowl or piece of meat.

2 crusts:
7-1/2 cups flour
2 cups + 4 tablespoons
    shortening
1-1/3 cups water
2 eggs
3 teaspoons salt

Sift flour and salt into a large bowl. Cut the shortening into the flour (as above). Add water to eggs and beat well; sprinkle over dough and mix in very quickly and lightly.

Then proceed as with other crusts.

PASTRY CRUST FOR MEAT PIES

This frontier crust is for meat pies, when raised bread dough is not used.

For two pies:
4 cups flour
1/4 teaspoon baking powder
pinch salt
1 cup lard
6-8 tablespoons cold water
   (approximately)

Sift together dry ingredients and cut in the lard as described above. Use as little water as possible to form into a ball and chill briefly.

For a richer crust, put small dabs of butter or lard on the dough before rolling to the desired size. For a lovely brown color, brush tops of pies with a mixture of eggs and milk or milk only and set immediately into a hot oven. This recipe was particularly favored because the baking powder addition permitted the use of less shortening.

DRIED FRUITS AND VEGETABLES

Miss Beecher wrote that "with a little skill and calculation, a housekeeper may contrive to keep a constant change of agreeable varieties on her table." In general, all fruits and berries, beans and squashes were dried and hung away, usually in paper bags and in a cool, dry place. Fruit leather was extremely popular with invalids and children, we are told. It is, moreover, a simple way to store a surplus of fruits.

PEACH LEATHER

Squeeze out the pulp of very ripe peaches, and spread it about half an inch thick (or less) on large platters; it should dry in the sun until quite hard and tough. Then roll up in layers with paper between each.

TOMATO LEATHER

Tomato leather is made in much the same way as peach. First pour boiling water over ripe tomatoes and peel them. Pour the pulp into a heavy kettle and cook briskly until it is reduced by half. For each gallon of pulp add 1 cup sugar and 1 tablespoon salt. Then spread the pulp on platters and dry for about 8-10 days in the sun and fresh air. (Pulp may also be spread on baking tins and dried in the oven.) Store in layers with paper between.
To cook the dried tomato leather, stew long and slowly in a good deal of water, adding bread crumbs and seasoning to taste.
What were called "tomato figs" were peeled, dried tomatoes spread out in the sun with sugar sprinkled over generously. They were packed with layers of sugar in between.

INDIAN "LEATHER BRITCHES BEANS"

Pick the green beans when young and string them on heavy thread, like long beads, one after the other. Hang the lines in a sunny place to dry thoroughly. It may take as long as a month or even two. When dried, store in baskets for winter use. To use, wash the beans well and soak 2 cups dried beans in 2 quarts of water for an hour or so. Add 1/4 pound diced salt pork, salt and pepper. Bring to a boil and reduce heat. Stir, then simmer very gently for at least 3 hours or until beans are tender, adding boiling water if needed to keep them from burning. They were served hot as a vegetable with the broth or "pot likker" on the side. Corn bread or corn pone was usually served with them.

APPLE LEATHER

Wash fresh ripe apples, then core and peel them. Put into a large saucepan and add enough water to half cover the fruit. Cook until reduced and very thick, then spread out on a clean cloth, a platter or a marble slab and let dry. It may take 2-3 days. Roll up in layers—sugar may or may not be sprinkled over each layer, with paper between.

DRIED APPLES

Peel but do not core the apples, then cut horizontally into thick slices—about 3/4-inch thick. Toss into a pan of salted cold water for a few hours. String the rings on long thin cord or yarn (like beads) and hang up the strings to dry from rafter over a fireplace or in the attic. Reconstituted, these make excellent pies in winter. Or soak until very soft, in cold water; add sugar and cook as applesauce.

Pumpkins and other hard-shelled squash may be dried in the same manner.

CANDLES AND SOAP

"Take a stick, wrap it firmly with moss, apply warm fat and let it harden around the moss . . . then wind about this, say, fiber or wicking."

This was one of the ingenious ways frontier people used to light their way.

Bear grease, deer suet, spermaceti (the solid wax from the head of a sperm whale) and, of course, New England bayberries were among the many materials used for making candles. The latter was by far the best; made of the boiled greenish wax of the berry, it did not melt easily, was impervious to warm weather, was not greasy to the touch and so fragrant that it served as a deodor-ant in stuffy, smoky rooms. Later, beeswax was heated and pressed around the wick, but these candles were considered expensive and were saved for company occasions. There was also the "tallow dip" in which wicks attached to sticks were dipped into well-rendered mutton fat.

Mrs. Child advises that "very hard and durable candles are made in the following manner: Melt together ten ounces of mutton tallow, a quarter of an ounce of camphor, four ounces of beeswax, and two ounces of alum. Candles made of these materials burn with a very clear light."

BAYBERRY CANDLES

Pick all twigs from the berries very carefully; then put them into a strainer and shake to remove any dust. Place the berries in a large kettle of water, large enough so they will float to the top, and set to the back of the stove (not on direct heat or the sediment will cook to wax) and leave overnight. In the morning, put into a cold place, preferably outdoors, so the wax may form into a solid mass; this should take a full day. Remove wax, put into a small kettle of water and again set to the back of the stove, not on direct heat.

When completely melted, strain through cheesecloth and again put outdoors to harden. The wax must be completely clean—if not, rewarm again and re-strain; keep it warm or it will harden before wanted.

The wax is now ready to be poured into molds or to dip by hand. Be sure wicks are much longer than the mold you are using so the candles may be pulled out. Place the wick in the mold; dip the top of it in warm wax and let it harden. Then pour in the wax. (Using a pitcher or teapot will make the pouring easier.) Be sure the mold is upright, or tie it to a faucet or other solid object, and let stand for about 8-12 hours. Then loosen the candle at the base with a sharp pointed object, and pull it out. If it does not come out easily, the wax was not completely clean; you may have to pour hot water over it to loosen it from the mold; if so, hold until firm again before laying down the candle.

10 pounds bayberries
    make 1 pound wax
1 pound wax makes
    2 large candles.

SOAPMAKING

Every frontier household made soap for its own use, and continued to do so in many parts of this country until well into the last quarter of the 19th century. But as communities grew, householders exchanged their wood ashes and accumulated fats for manufactured soap; and when coal and oil replaced wood for heating and cooking, the practice was generally abandoned.

Like many other frontier tasks, soapmaking was a continuing activity. All year round the huge lye barrel, with its perforated bottom, stood outside the kitchen door to catch the good clean ashes from stoves and fireplaces. Underneath it was the lye basin, used to catch the lye drippings as rainwater strained through the ashes. To get the lye good and strong, the basin was often emptied back into the barrel. In gauging the strength of the lye, they used to say that it should "bear up an egg, or a potato, so that you can see a piece of the surface as big as a ninepence. . . . If it sinks, it is too weak and if it floats half way in the liquid, it is too strong, just as bad . . . ."

The best time to make soap was immediately after the annual slaughtering; large quantities of animal fat was then available.

The usual proportion was 3 pounds grease to a pailful of lye. Thrown into the kettle over a brisk fire, it was boiled until all impurities floated to the top—to be discarded—and the soap was thick and "ropy." Then it was carried indoors, usually downcellar, and poured into a barrel so all superfluous liquid could drain off. The soap was put into boxes or molds to harden and cut into convenient pieces.

Cold soap was made without boiling. The fats were rendered and strained and the lye prepared. They were mixed together, set out in the sun and stirred often during the ensuing 5-6 days.

SOFT SOAP

1 13-ounce can lye
1 quart cold water
1 tablespoon ammonia
2 tablespoons borax
6 pounds fat (left from kitchen uses)

Using a large stoneware crock or an enamel pan (uncovered metal cannot be used), mix the lye and cold water *with great care,* for if it splashes on the hands it will burn. It will heat up, so stir very gently until it cools, then add the ammonia and borax.

In a large kettle (iron is best) melt down the fat and set aside to cool.

In a slow steady stream, pour lye mixture into the fat, *stirring constantly but gently* with a long smooth stick. Continue stirring as it thickens and when quite thick, pour into a mold or a long shallow box. Before it hardens, cut into convenient bars. It is best left to age a few weeks.

To make hard soap, cover while still hot with a salt brine made of 1 tablespoon salt to each gallon of water; the soap will rise to the top. Skim off when cooled and cut into bars. Set aside to age.

A FINE HAND SOAP

3 cups coconut oil
3 cups olive or mineral oil
4-3/4 cups mutton fat
1 quart cold water
1 13-ounce can lye

In a large enamel kettle, mix all the fats and heat until they become a clear liquid. In a stoneware crock or enamel kettle, mix the cold water and lye and stir constantly—*slowly and smoothly to avoid splashing*—until it cools. Slowly pour lye solution into the warm liquid grease, stirring steadily. When it thickens, pour into molds or a shallow wooden box and cool. Cut into convenient bars and age for a few weeks, at least. It makes a rich, fine soap which may be used on the face.

TO CLARIFY FAT

Measure the fat you plan to use (beef or other animal fat), add an equal volume of water to it and bring to a boil, reduce heat and simmer until liquid. Remove from heat. Stir well and add a little cold water which will make impurities sink to the bottom.

INDEX

INDEX

189

BIBLIOGRAPHY

Beecher, Miss Catherine, *Domestic Receipt Book*, New York, 1846

Benson, Evelyn Anrahan (Ed.), *Penn Family Recipes* (recipes of Wm. Penn's wife, Gulielma, 1644-94), New York 1966

Child, Mrs. Lydia Maria, *The American Frugal Housewife, Dedicated to Those Who are Not Ashamed of Economy*, Boston 1832

Kitchiner, William, M.D., *The Cook's Oracle and Housekeeper's Manual...*, New York 1830 (London, 1817)

Moritz, Mrs. C.F. and Kahn, Miss Adele, *The Twentieth Century Cook Book*, New York 1879

Neill, Miss E., *The Every-Day Cook-Book*, San Francisco, 1889

Randolph, Mrs. Mary, *The Virginia Housewife*, Baltimore, 1836

Simmons, Amelia, *American Cookery*, A Facsimile of the 1st Edition, 1796. New York 1958

Tyree, Marion Cabell, *Housekeeping in Old Virginia*, Louisville, Ky. 1879

Wright, Mrs. Julia McNair, *The Com Complete Home: an Encylopedia of Domestic Life and Affairs . . . a volume of Practical Experiences Popularly Illustrated*, A. L. Bancroft, San Francisco, 1879

Farmers' Almanack, 1839

The American Family Cook Book (Author, Publisher and Date Unknown)

BIOGRAPHICAL NOTES

In the sense that she describes "pioneer" as the amalgamation of Old World customs with the new, Gertrude Harris herself was raised in a pioneer family. Her parents were Russian Jews who emigrated to New York, and adapted their European culinary heritage to the means and ingredients available in metropolitan America. Mrs. Harris first encountered the pioneer tradition of "making do" in New York during World War II, when she and her husband, the painter-sculptor Zev, had to use their ingenuity to feed a constant deluge of house guests on limited wartime rations. Like the pioneer women of whom she writes with such empathy, Mrs. Harris moved west to California after the war and began incorporating the produce and seafoods of the Pacific into her East Coast/European repertoire of recipes. To complete the full circle, Gertrude Harris moved to Europe, lived in Rome and Paris during the 1950's and again combined the culinary ways of a new country—this time that of the Old World—into her own heritage.

Mrs. Harris' formal training is actually in the arts. She received a bachelor's degree in art education from New York University and has directed galleries of contemporary art in New York City, Monterey (California) and Rome. Her art reviews have appeared in various journals in the United States and abroad and her poetry has been published in several anthologies, including *53 American Poets*, edited by Ruth Witt-Diamant and published by Kenkyusha, Japan.

This is Gertrude Harris' second book for 101 Productions. Her *Pots & Pans, Etc.*, a guide and critique of various cookware, was published in 1971. Previously she had edited *Picnic-in-the-Point-Park* cookbook, published by the Contra Costa Shoreline Parks Committee as a fund-raiser for a Save the San Francisco Bay campaign—an indication of the vital concern with ecology which is so evident in this present volume. In the San Francisco area Mrs. Harris is also a well-known authority on herbs. In her own garden in Point Richmond, northeast of San Francisco, she raises most of the common and many unusual varieties of herbs. She has conducted herb lectures and "taste-ins" throughout the area.

The research for *Manna: Foods of the Frontier* actually began shortly after the Harrises moved to California when Gertrude began collecting historic cookbooks as reference material for a recipe book on chicken and eggs. The scope of this project was broadened as Mrs. Harris became deeply involved with the epic story of the pioneer women. This book is the result of the research of nearly thirty years—collecting old recipes, testing them and adapting them to modern tastes and methods.